"Your poems are serious and full of passion. I am interested that you taught philosophy for a time. I hope you will write more poetry about Stonehenge." letter to Carolyn Grassi from Iris Murdoch, renowned novelist

Journey to Chartres is the next best thing to a season in France. How much is evoked and put into the most luminous of perspectives. These are truly refreshing poems.
James Merrill, renowned poet

Carolyn Grassi's collection of poems: *Transparencies* contains so many richly remembered scenes of people and places, cultural landmarks and sacred sites. A fine union of poetic sensibility and psychological insight.
Dr. Joseph Henderson, co-founder of SF Jung Institute

At the heart of Carolyn Grassi's odyssey into the past and present is the simple, pulsing lyric instinct: to hold experience like a live bird in her hands. Her adventures through art and grief return us again and again to memory's golden treasure– still, bright and abiding."
J.D. McClatchy, poet, regarding *Transparencies*

Carolyn Grassi's collection of poems *Heart and Soul* charts a personal and spiritual autobiography in plain language that sings and is deeply resonant and moving.
John Ashbery, renowned poet

In *Heart and Soul, Poems* you will find the stages of a New World pilgrim's progress. There's a fascinating narrative holding these lyric pieces together: a history seen through the eyes of a clear-sighted and compassionate woman, a veritable song of myself from another Brooklyn poet.
Paul Mariani, poet and biographer

Other books by Carolyn Grassi:

Poetry:

HEART AND SOUL
(Patmos Press, SF)

TRANSPARENCIES
(Patmos Press, SF)

JOURNEY TO CHARTRES
(Black Swan Books, CT)

Spirituality:

*MARY MAGDALENE AND
THE WOMEN IN JESUS' LIFE*
co-authored with Joseph Grassi
(Sheed and Ward)

BROOKLYN
BEGINNINGS

Poems by Carolyn Grassi

Patmos Press
San Francisco, California

Published by Patmos Press,
San Francisco, California

ISBN: 978-0-9742435-2-8
Library of Congress Cataloging-in-Publication Data
Grassi, Carolyn   Brooklyn Beginnings, Poems

Cover design by Tom Fenton
Text of this book set in Book Antiqua 11 point
First Edition
Printed in the United States of America

ACKNOWLEDGMENTS AND DEDICATION

This book of poems is dedicated with love and thanks to my grandchildren, Madeline and Ethan Grassi, son Eddie Grassi and daughter-in-law Shalini Kaushik-Grassi, son Peter Grassi, my late husband, Joseph Grassi, my late parents, Edwin and Betty Cook, my brothers, John Cook and his family, and the late Richard Cook and his family, our grandparents, Florence and Reginald Ball, Florence and John Cook, Margaret Drury.

I wish to thank and acknowledge longtime friend and gifted poet, James Torrens S.J., for his proof reading and invaluable editorial advice offered with wit and wisdom all the way. Abundant thanks to the fine publishing team of Tom Fenton and Mary Heffron. I am grateful to A. David Moody, Professor emeritus at the University of York (UK), for editorial encouragement from the beginning of this project.

Many thanks to friends, near and far, for whom the final poem is dedicated. My gratitude to Mary Jeanne Oliva, Betty Steidel, and Pushpa MacFarlane for assistance during this challenging time of a pandemic. I am grateful for mentors, teachers, friends in the Maryknoll communities, Brooklyn College CUNY, San Jose State University, the C.G. Jung Institute and the Analytical Psychology Club in San Francisco, the San Jose Poetry Center, Chinese Medicine Works Acupuncture, San Francisco, and for the Noe Valley Ministry Presbyterian Church, San Francisco.

I believe within us reside living presences, some cultures name as our ancestors, bestowed by the Divine, who wish to be recalled and companion us as guides on Life's journey. May you, dear reader, celebrate and continue discovering your unique being on this beautiful planet as linked with all creatures past, present, and into the future.

"The Word is a living, being, spirit, all verdant
greening, all creativity. This Word manifests
itself in every creature."
Hildegard of Bingen (1098-1179)

"Recognition of the shadow leads to the modesty we
need in order to acknowledge imperfection. A human
relationship is not based on differentiation and perfection,
for these only emphasize the differences or call forth the
exact opposite; it is based, rather, on imperfection, on what
is weak, helpless and in need of support - the very ground
and motive of dependence. The perfect has no need of the
other, but weakness has, for it seeks support and does not
confront its partner with anything that might force him/her
into an inferior position and even humiliate him/her. This
humiliation may happen only too easily where idealism
plays too prominent a role."
C.G. Jung "The Undiscovered Self"

I. BEGINNINGS IN BROOKLYN

II. THE BODY POLITIC

III. HOMAGES: PEOPLE, PLACES

PEOPLE

PLACES

IV. SPIRITS GALORE

V. ALCHEMY

Postscript
in thanks to the Sisters of Charity,
and in memory of all the girls who lived
at Saint Joseph's Home, Brooklyn, New York

I. BEGINNINGS IN BROOKLYN

FIRST SNOW, FIRST COMMUNION

. . . first memory of snow I was very young
    struggling as I climbed the couch pressing
my face against the window of our apartment
    thrilled to see tiny white circles tumbling
from the sky a shimmery blanket covering
    our old car by the curb so bundled warmly
Dad carried me outside saying: "See the snow!"
    as a shower of little stars were falling from
heaven melting on my face tasting cold turning
    warm on my tongue swallowing something
magical followed a few years later by First
    Communion at Holy Cross Church Brooklyn
as I hummed a hymn seeing the Sacred Host
    held high then tasted the wafer melt in my
mouth feeling God's presence pouring into me
    that May day akin though differently to a cold
December night looking up in wonder at snow
    flurries coming into my life for the first time . . .

MORNING GLORIES

green vines blue flowering trumpets by
a No Parking sign bordering a chain-link
fence at the corner of Steiner and California

in San Francisco as I lingered by gleaming
glories peeking through fog by a construction
site reviving memories of a wild backyard

behind the fence of Jack's grocery store on
Lott Street in Brooklyn beside our family's
apartment when I went with my brothers

Richie and John climbing over cut glass
and a barbed wire barrier we shimmied
down into high weeds trying to avoid

thorns in rose bushes within this forbidden
place where we played Hide 'n Seek by
hydrangeas jumped over old tires and

squishy garbage in dirt by our sneakers
soon the owner shouted from the top floor
"Get out or I'll call the cops!" running fast

we scaled the fence and broken glass bottles
bypassing morning glories who were waving
blue petaled trumpets cheering us on and over

THE OTHER SIDE OF FLATBUSH

1.

ah summer afternoons as an eleven year old
   I often rode my bike to the other side of
Flatbush wishing my family lived in one
   of those lovely homes with lawns watered
by a sprinkler and you could eat ice cream
   on a porch during hot days or play board
games at a table in the living room with a view
   of maple trees out front and wondered how

it was having a piano as I often heard people
    playing near an open window and of course
I loved looking at gardens lined with roses
    to pick for a bouquet to give my mother . . .

                    2.
. . . many years later I mentioned this beautiful
section of Brooklyn to my mother such a surprising
    story she shared: "Oh that's where I grew up in
a lovely home owned by Uncle Howard, who let
    my family, that is your grandparents, raise me
and my brother there on one condition: that we
    children attend Catholic school, since he was
a recent convert and wanted us to follow him into
    the church, as the expression was in those days.
School was wonderful since the nuns were extra
    kind to me saying they prayed that I'd convert,
which I did at 15, then my brother, father and at
    last my mother, who converted reluctantly as
she loved the small Protestant community where
    we worshipped compared to the large Catholic
parish we joined. Soon after I got a job in the city,
    Uncle Howard sold that beautiful home, so we
moved to an apartment on the other side of Flatbush."

                    3.
another anecdote to this story of the girl
I was daydreaming of the lovely homes in
    what was once upon a time my mother's
neighborhood and then pedaling back to
    our rented railroad room flat without
windows in the bedrooms and an upstairs
    landlord shouting at us kids if we dared
step a foot in his scroungy tiny front yard
    yet we were wonderfully blest by a magical
beautiful local parish church with magnificent

murals and a sanctuary filled on feast days
with candles flowers incense and a mysterious
    marvelous sounding Latin language then
after Mass we walked home under an archway
    of gorgeous maples alongside the church . . .

CAMP OH-NEH-TAH, EAST WINDHAM, NEW YORK

As a child I loved summer camp in the Catskills
a cabin bed beside an open window surrounded
by birches maples pines elms aspens city girls

playing sports in a meadow swimming in Silver
Lake encircled by forests waving over the water
easy to see storm clouds rising across the valley

at the top of Hunter Mountain at times hurricanes
breached the dining room perched as it was above
a cliff we'd hear water rushing wildly for a week

till at last the sun slipped around Mount Zorn
sending spears of golden light with a rainbow
warming everything in sight bluebells shaking

off rain sparrows chirping crows calling chickens
clucking on the farm beyond the field and damp
earth steaming as we crowded round the campfire

moon bright beside blinking stars each camper's
eyes sparkling colorful blankets drawn close round
our shoulders we headed to bed jumping over

puddles slipping on stones wet bushes brushing
our legs skipping up cabin steps boots left
on porch kerosene lamps shimmering shadows

4

we curled up in cots falling asleep serenaded
by forest murmurs quaking aspens whistling
pines north star serenely seen sky clear of clouds

STONES, MARBLES

1.

following an ancient custom I sometimes
   place a pink stone from Aberdeen's North
Sea at the foot of my bed for a favorable dream
   imagining it was washed ashore near where
great-grandpa Skea captained Cunard ships
   since recalling our people's legendary origins
among the Orkney Islands' myths of humans
   mating with sea creatures perpetuated by
grandma when whispering the "family secret"
   of her sister Nancy's two webbed toes linking
us to "silkies" since such was so-called proof

2.

as kids growing up in Flatbush Brooklyn
   we saved pocket money to buy marbles
for trading and playing within chalk circles
   we drew in the street one at a time taking
aim to win a swirling sea blue agate a green
   forestry globe an orange orb streaked by
lightning bolts meaning we guessed each
   marble might possess a secret aura within
that seemed to call on our skills to bring home
   a treasure thanks to speed accuracy grace
as our young hands tried to focus and win
   one or more magical presences containing
up close stars suns moons planets earths
   crystal-balls held in small palms sometimes
placed in socks perhaps later rubbed for luck

3.

after entering the British Museum Joe and I
   sought and found the Rosetta Stone not far
from the entrance standing strong in darkened
   splendor of the ages and countless rubbings
since a codex deciphering alchemical formulas
   embedded in hieroglyphics a stone's throw
as it were away from the Elgin Marbles' carvings
   of communities in processions beside animals
wearing garlands to a sacrificial fate we followed
   silently into a large chamber where a goddess
presided as centuries ago in Greece's marble
   Parthenon overseeing the Athenian Acropolis

BEGINNINGS IN BROOKLYN

an after-life: yes, no, maybe, beliefs vary, even for Catholics
   who sometimes cast about in doubtful categories taught in
childhood: portraits of Limbo, Hell, and Purgatory: gate-way
   to Paradise, some mistakenly think we grew up in "fear
and trembling" about "eternal damnation" if we committed
   a mortal sin and died before formally confessing contrition,
not to worry, since an all-forgiving God was preached in
   my childhood's Brooklyn parish, no matter your offense,
crucial at the end is express regretful sorrow without needing
   to say the words aloud if no chance for formal Confession,
enough if expressed in your heart so opening flood-gates of
   mercy, forgiveness flowing in a faith felt for a loving God
made tangible by our family's fantastic father's kindness
   merging with a sense of a loving Deity, plus parish priests
living what they preached: good will to all and joyful singing
   Irish ballads at church dances, no wonder we three kids
thought about entering "religious life," though my brothers
   married, I joined a missionary community, unfortunately
assigned to count money for the men's wing, so I left and

married, over time trying to recall divinity's diversity
in persons, places, communities, callings as with poetry

BROOKLYN RUMBLINGS

1.
. . . whenever Dad drove us back to Brooklyn
   through the city's Bowery often a homeless man
knocked on the car window, hoping for a handout
   and I'd wonder if this was my great-grandfather,
John Ball, who lost his wealth during the depression,
   so disappeared from the family. Perhaps the tale
played an unconscious part in my choosing to enter
   a convent that served oppressed outsiders. Grandpa
Reginald and grand-Uncle Howard inherited their
   father's "baggage," but differently, both held steady
jobs at New York Insurance companies. Grandpa was
   addicted to card games, maybe a wish to win back
money his father lost in stocks, while Howard never
   married and devoted himself to their mother, while
hoarding wealth, perhaps fearing financial insecurity,
   though taking solace in conversion to Catholicism
plus an attempt to atone for his father's abandoning
   the family in seeking forgiveness for supposed "sins
of the father" by leaving $100,000 to the church's Society
   for the Propagation of the Faith; I'll never know if he
donated to the Catholic Worker caring for the homeless . . .

2.
my brothers and I were born and raised in Flatbush,
   a neighborhood of recently arrived southern Blacks,
immigrant Irish, Italians, and Jews, not far from Sears,
   A&P, Merkel's market, Hunt's Fish, Woolworth's,
Thom McAn's, Fanny Farmers, Loew's Kings Theatre,
   RKO Kenmore, Chinese take-out on Church Avenue,
buses, subways, bikes, walking, Mom bought clothes

at Gimbels basement and Thrift shops, we played
at public parks and beaches, summer camps sponsored
    by the Herald Tribune Fresh Air Fund for kids from
New York City's five boroughs, I went with African-
American, Puerto Rican, and Irish girls, every one
treated equally, sharing cabins, sports, hikes etcetera;
    predominantly white counselors, two Black Baptists,
Miss Shirley, Miss Gwen, one Jewish Miss Colette
    and Catholic Miss Mary from NYC's Hell's Kitchen;
at age 14 I learned counseling skills by living with
    Miss Shirley, who taught by example and advice
ways to instill confidence in each girl and the group,
    so we'd feel like family in sharing chores, playing
cards on rainy days, singing dawn to dusk, talking
    over the day's activities and what hikes to sign up
for tomorrow; tears and hugs, hard saying goodbye,
    summer's end when Miss Shirley returned to Ohio

BLESSED BROOKLYN COUPLE
in memory of Mary and John Hanley

Always a warm welcome from Mrs. Hanley when
    I knocked on the door: "It's so good to see you.
Come on in." A baby around her hip as she warmed
    a bottle on the stove. Mr. Hanley, a gentle-man,
postal-carrier never missed a day of work. He took
    Judy, Barbara, and me to our first movie, asking us
to remove all wrappers from candy boxes, so not to
    disturb patrons. Parties galore at the Hanley's home,
my family and other neighbors celebrating countless
    Baptisms, First Communions, Confirmations, school
graduations. A keg of beer, sodas, pretzels, potato chips
    in the kitchen. Mr. Hanley opened the evening with
"Oh, Danny Boy!" We girls performed dance routines
    to popular records. All the while Mrs. Hanley smiled
as she cared for her widowed mother, relatives, friends,

her husband, the eleven kids, plus any guests who
dropped in. One Spring day Judy, Barbara, Jane, Winnie,
   Kathy, Frances, and I walked with Mrs. Hanley pushing
the carriage to Prospect Park. She spread a sheet under
   a maple tree, served sodas, chips, peanut butter and
jelly sandwiches. We wove wildflowers for her lovely
   blonde hair, singing and dancing in a circle, while happily
crowning her our Queen of the May, as she fed baby Jackie.

FALLING IN LOVE, PROSPECT PARK BROOKLYN
in memory of my parents, Eddie and Betty Cook

. . . years after Dad died, I discovered his letter
   saying "as a young man on a cold winter's night
I went with friends for fun to Prospect Park and
   what a wonderful sight, a beautiful woman
wearing a white fluffy hat with black hair blowing
   in the wind, laughing while sleigh-riding down
a steep hill. And she became your mother. That's
   why I've loved that park for our family! Spring
playing baseball on Lookout Hill, summer rowing
   round the lake, visiting the zoo, sleigh-riding too!"
So the park became a magnet drawing me back with
   my brothers and friends, summer days exploring
side-paths, bridges, hills, discovering the Vale of
   Cashmere where grandpa and Uncle Howard
played checkers on a stone table in the Rose Garden;
   Dad driving us through the park to visit relatives;
Judy and I riding bikes to meet grandma on the hill
   overlooking Long Meadow on to the zoo's polar
bears, lions, elephants, deer, giraffes, seals; riding
   the Flatbush bus by-passing the park on my way
to high school downtown near the Brooklyn Bridge;
   now holding Dad's letter, I see that snowy night,
his falling in love at first sight for a beautiful woman
   laughing as she was sleigh-riding to Swan Lake . . .

SCOTTISH SELKIE ANCESTORS
in memory of grandma, Florence Skea Ball

Aberdeen's pink granite stone facades shimmer
    over old and newer neighborhoods. This was
my grandmother's city, Saint Machar's church,
    where she worshiped. Her father captained
ships bound for the Far East. She sang "Bye yon
    Bonnie Banks" while brushing my hair. She
kept the secret of her half-sister Nancy born with
    two webbed toes, saving this news on meeting
my brother's fiancée, prefacing her announcement
    with "I think you ought to know this." A sigh of
relief from my future sister-in-law, who told me
    this story, saying: "Two webbed toes were not
the worst thing in the world!" Legends say such
    anomalies are a sign of a selkie (human/seal).
Now grandpa was a serious man uninterested in
    Scottish lore, so he'd say "Flo, we already heard
that!" but I'd beg her to tell me more! Sometimes
    I've wondered if in the old days did the family
look first at a baby's feet? Was I checked at birth
    by grandma? No descendants of the Orkneys with
webbed toes except Aunt Nancy as far as I know,
    though this family history may explain why I feel
an affinity for myths featuring sea-creatures. Can
    webbed toes develop later in life; silly selkie self
thinking such a thought! though I admit wondering
    although I only tiptoed in the North Sea once . . .

NOVITIATE AFFIRMATION
in memory of Sister Celestine M.M.

Once upon a time many years ago in the convent,
    Sister Celestine's comment: "You remind me of
Lord Tennyson." Totally ignorant of who he was,

nevertheless, I sensed a compliment, uncommon
     as it was, since we were trained to always think
first and last of others, never oneself, yet she dared

praise my poem on a Thanksgiving montage that
     she assigned me for the library bulletin board,
so something worthwhile in my stanzas mixed in

the cornucopia theme becoming a turning point
     since she played a major part with her words,
while raising an index finger saying: "Why yes,

like Tennyson" whom I never read, so searched
     for him in the encyclopedia, though it would
be years before I'd read his poetry, not a favorite,

yet ancestral spirit thanks to Sister linking me to
     him via my poem becoming a crucial turning
point in my life due to her disobeying the Rule

discouraging any personal praise, though over
     time a kinship for Tennyson dove-tailed with
my Scottish grandmother's love of legends as

the Lady of the Lake, King Arthur's Round Table,
     Guinevere, Galahad, Merlin, stories she spoke
of enthusiastically as beloved folklore in Scotland,

so decades later, far from home, in a cloistered
     Massachusetts novitiate, I lapped up words of
Sister Celestine empowering me to write poetry,

thus preparing my call into that art with thanks
     to her as I work this poem listening to Loreena
McKennitt singing Tennyson's "The Lady of Shalott."

NOVITIATE, TOPSFIELD, MASSACHUSETTS

a lawn behind the cloistered novitiate was where
    chairs were set on certain Sundays for families
to visit their daughters, though in hindsight I regret
    never thinking how long a drive from Brooklyn
for my parents, toss in the strict Canonical year rule:
    only two family visits in a year and not from friends;
the goal I suppose preparation for missionary work,
    i.e. five years away from the U.S. serving the poor
in developing countries, best become adaptable to
    privations as a practice wherever we went, detach
from past attachments, accept whoever was assigned
    to live with you; I did love the novitiate location
surrounded by a forest teeming with birches, pines,
    elms, maples, laurels, willows, and the aroma of
winter firesides from nearby homes, not hidden by
    summer trees, so see smoke rise on clear crisp days,
making me long for a home in the country; though
    I never mentioned that to anyone, since few chances
to confide in a friend with "The Rule" hanging over
    affection, that is: "No talking in twos" to prevent
the forbidden label of "a particular friendship," though
    I dared disobey the taboo behind backs of my superiors
for the sake of sisters I loved in those pre-liberal Vatican II
    times when the bell ended family visits, quick goodbyes
then off to chapel for chanting psalms across the aisle,
    though six years later this chapter in my life ended
on feeling called to leave and marry someone I came
    to meet at the complementary community of men
at the seminary near our motherhouse down the road . . .

BLUE BIRD CALLING, OSSINING, NEW YORK

gray-blue Palisades cliffs covered with green woods
    overlooking the Hudson River across from our
convent's apple orchard bordered by a field of wild

flowers delightful after chanting Vespers in chapel
I was standing on the deck following a rain shower
   listening to a blue bird singing on a branch close
enough to see light shining within wet feathers
   while the tiny throat trembled as each note rose
in joy till day went down over the hills at sunset and
   I felt this little one was a messenger as if an angel
calling me back into the world so on my way to bed
   I hummed the Pentecostal hymn "Come Holy Spirit
Creator blest and in our hearts take up Your rest" yes
   Love's dove disguised in a blue bird's tongue fired
song bringing me back to Brooklyn marriage a family
   eventually we'd fly United airlines all the way west . . .

SEVEN LAKES REGION, NEW YORK

Harriman State Park New York, where Joe and I
   often hiked decades later my niece Colleen drove
me to her father's (my brother's) nearby home she
   rounded a bend along Seven Lakes Drive such
a sudden sweeping view of Lake Tiorati's blue
   gleaming waters flanked by a once-upon-a-time
familiar pine forest waving as if a long-lost friend
   perhaps recalling when I came with Joe crossing
Bear Mountain Bridge in his VW Bug then eagerly
   a familiar trail hike for our site to set up the tent
near maples though that was long ago this time
   snow blanketed the woods yet sweet familiar
pine scent mingling with bird calls coming across
   from the other shore while brilliant golden leaves
still asleep till they burst beautiful in Spring as it
   was when so in love we rolled under their canopy

ANGELS OF MERCY

1.

as a child I learned lessons about angels who
    supposedly appear with or without asking,
so at age ten alongside classmates lining up for
    Confirmation, suddenly Sister in charge shouted:
*"Why are you wearing socks, when you were told
    to wear stockings today! Go home and change."*
"No one is home! They've already left for church."
    "Just go!" Sobbing I rushed out the side door,
soon stopped by Mrs. Armstrong, mother of a girl
    in class, whom I hardly knew. She gently asked
what was wrong then said: *"Quick! Come with me!"*
    So she hailed a cab and off we rushed to a shop
that sold stockings. I pulled them on as the taxi
    rushed back to the church, just in time, as I was
fourth in the procession line of forty girls for
    Confirmation, soon seeing my family smiling
across the aisle. I couldn't see Mrs. Armstrong
    in the crowd, but felt her presence closer than
any angel in the sanctuary's Resurrection mural . . .

2.

. . . grace-filled unexpected blessings come
    when needed as the cafe clerk conveying
concern: *"How have you been? I haven't seen
    you in a while."* Or at the car shop, a mechanic
offers a discount coupon I knew nothing about.
    And at my grandkids' school several times
a week the crossing monitor greets me warmly
    with: *"Cómo estás?"* so we share family stories.
Early evening the bell rings and neighbor Hercilia
    brings a bowl of her homemade Brazilian rice
pudding. Aware I'm a widow, she offers to pick up
    anything at the grocery store. More surprises too

14

out of the blue, as manna from heaven answering
   our prayers, good news carried angel wings by
an extraordinary kind editor saying he will bring
   my book's finale to publication. Always I bow to
you, dear reader, for purchasing and reading poetry,
   so rebirthing arts at the homes of hearts and souls,
since after all is said and done, artists like crafts-folk
   ages ago added unique talents to the whole work of
creating a cathedral, though anonymously given gifts
   in a grace-filled glorious co-op overcoming ego, grief
and grave with hope-filled harmonizing placement
   within a loving community. This note comes from
a San Jose California homeless shelter to volunteers:
   "Thank you for your kindness to strangers.
   You may be entertaining angels."

SILVER LININGS

Rustling winds through open windows as a darling dove's
   descending in the story mingling divinity's desire with
creatures conceiving planets/earth dawn/dusk east/
   west north/south land/sea you/me we/they us/other
spring/shore work/play tales spinning webs weaving
   touch downs time and again in our ordinary lives lilies
of the fields neither toil nor reap yet blest beautifully as also
   lovely lavender laurels roses daffodils dandelions arches
of rainbows after storms in city gutters skyscrapers glisten
   after storms a lamb leading flocks into peaceful pastures
people choosing a plant-based diet climate change starts
   at our table choices pardon my preaching it's taken me
a while to make the connection methane from animals in
   crowded factory farms emitting high amounts of green-
house gases finally many folks trying teriyaki baked tofu
   tastes like chicken quinoa is becoming popular silver
linings during a pandemic more people walking in Nature

BLISSFUL START-UPS

Yes bring back blissful memories of marvelous
start-ups we've each known at the threshold
     a baby's tiny hands
clapping at seeing for the first time how lovely
the sun shone in maple leaves near where
     my father smiled
as he rocked the carriage and lifted weights
for his Saturday exercise perhaps a prelude
     at age ten awesome
sight of aspens quaking with summer light
through an open cabin window by my bed
     at camp's rest-hour
magical moment too atop Mount Zorn beside
city girls watching dawn slowly descend into
     the valley's lake
sunbeams rippling as once upon a time seeing
blissful leaves shimmering on a Brooklyn roof

HIGH SCHOOL CONFESSIONS
in memory of Natalie Budny

a flickering summer Saturday night memory:
   warm air rising from the street before and after
Natalie and I entered our parish church during
   high school years, when we'd laugh on line for
Confession, light a candle after praying a casual
   Penance at the altar, a ritual linking us with
every one else as flawed but fine, whatever faults,
   a fresh start since forgiven felt good, best of all
rewarding ourselves with an ice-cream soda at
   a favorite hangout on Nostrand Avenue, where
we went when I was full of hope to see Jimmy
   walk nearby our booth, he being the boy I fell
for in fourth grade when he paraded with his class

in the school auditorium for social dance lessons
once a week, Natalie always understood how I felt,
    as I did her crush on someone unattainable too,
so we daydreamed aloud together yet eventually
    changed our affections on to Christ completely
leading us to enter different convents, so a final
    farewell and sadly she died too young, but what
fun we had remains indelibly inscribed in my heart

EAST AND WEST
in memory of Joseph Grassi

your warm glance dark eyes intelligent
    thoughtful forehead enchanting smile
plus an air of genuine spiritual closeness
    to Nature when we were young at heart
no matter our age at the start no burdens
    dating-hikes by the Palisades overlooking
the Hudson day-dreaming a future family
    of our own first finding a job out west
without forgetting those magical days in
    the first blush of love's linking bouquets
of maple leaves quaking aspens laurel
    groves ancient oaks willows waving as
we burrowed in a cave during a thunder
    storm while on an Appalachian Trail trek
through the Blue Ridge Mountains followed
    a few years later by migrating to California
discovering redwoods with sons Eddie and Peter
    hiking along the Pacific ridge zig-zag trail plus
hikes round Santa Clara valley's San Jose parks
    where we lived for decades not far from
the Santa Cruz mountain cabin you built in
    Ben Lomond for our family plus many
times we climbed the city by the Bay crossed

Golden Gate Bridge reached Mount Tamalpais
also ferry rides to Angel Island akin to our driving
over the Hudson River for Bear Mountain forests . . .

YOSEMITE FALLS WITH JOE

An eagle was soaring through mountain mists
    over ridges while Joe and I were walking beside
Merced River's aspens oaks birches willows elms

seeking the trailhead for our climb from the valley
    floor to the top of Yosemite's double waterfalls
so for several hours with walking sticks along

up a zigzag path stopping half way for a respite
    on a rocky ledge overlooking the lower falls
close enough for cool mists to cover our face

before hiking higher while every so often I'd ask:
    "How much longer?" Joe's patient reply: "We'll
be there soon." At last we reached the summit in

a half circle of pines waving a welcome beside
    hikers who greeted us as if forming a family
reunion along the large stone ledge under a blue

sky facing El Capitan as Joe leaned over the falls'
    misty rainbow tinted clouds rising as I called:
"Please come back. You're too close to the edge"

but ever the daring one he lingered asking me to
    look down and see where the falls joins Merced
River flowing together beyond the Ahwahnee and

Curry Village so it was surrounded by awesome
   beauty I asked "What do you believe happens
in an after-life?" spontaneously opening his arms

spread wide as an eagle embracing all he surveyed
   saying "Why we return to God in places like this
where Creation continually renews Life . . ." so we

held hands in a thanksgiving prayer before taking
   the trail down simple dinner at a communal table
early to bed love-making under moon and stars . . .

EASTER WEEK'S MEMORIES RISING
in memory of my brother Richie Cook

across San Francisco's Crissy Field Easter week
   memories rising I see Richie at that tough job
after high school barbequing chickens in a tiny
   store front on Flatbush Avenue his ever ready
smile even on sweltering days and always first
   to start games on our street with all the kids
his contagious child-like enthusiasm spinning
   through everything happy helping hands
for his employees assisting immigrants with
   jobs housing health education not one to
parade good deeds or complain about hard
   times following in our father's footsteps
in devoted every day loving care for family
   friends community sprinkling fun-filled
adventures with street-smarts working hard
   in that sweltering job as a high school kid
to help support our family I miss his witty
   wise words making me laugh through tears
with him at Easter morning in Holy Cross
   Church haven at home jumping for joy
Easter egg baskets trumpet blasting *Alleluias*

19

MOZART ON THE SAN MATEO BRIDGE

some folks as me in this post-modern 21st century
continue believing in blissful after-life reunions with
    deceased loved ones looking forward to my beloved
partner reviving years ago hiking the Palisades trail
    over-looking the Hudson River valley step by step
our synchronicity through thickets brushing aside
    brambles clothes torn by thorns bitten by bugs cut
by branches scented by lavender luckily not skunk
    spray happily forget-me-nots clinging to our clothes
pine scent in our hair we wore ponchos in New York
    rains unlike California's dry/wet seasons conjured
decades later as now driving solo across wind-swept
    San Mateo Bridge back to Pacifica connecting east/
west of San Francisco Bay while white-caps' spray rise
    below a blue sky brushed clouds fresh from the ocean
while flocks of seagulls swerve dip coast as I listen
    to a CD of Mozart's "Figaro" finale fill my car even
as jets hum close-by for an SFO landing the aria's
    crescendo of pardon/forgiveness/love everlasting
overcoming death up-ending farewells in a loving
    musical choir of climax playing across decade after
decade as if Mozart smiles in every line and note . . .
    promising we will/are/shall reach *alleluia reunions*

CALIFORNIA'S LIGHT AMAZED MY MOTHER
in memory of Mom, Betty Ball Cook

California's light amazed my mother during
    her first visit out west contrasting humid
shielding sun back east and a far cry from

grandma's North Sea's Orkney Island people
    who set stones aligned with the solstice so
to gather golden light in carved chalices after

20

long dark chilly days and nights welcoming
    warm wonder's return and who can say if
our souls become saturated by ancestral traces

archetypes rituals beliefs elementary stuff
    sticking as the legendary Middle Eastern
story of three friends following a star along

an ancient Silk Road to a Palestinian manger's
    divine child asleep on straw mixing markers
of travels tucked in stories of us earthlings

seeking hope for better times to come after
    months of harsh storms tearing through
countless lives grandma's tales of rough seas

that her father faced in captaining ships
    with immigrants leaving Liverpool for Lady
of Liberty's harbor settling down decades in

New York City till her daughter my mother
    a widow migrated west with me and our
family recreating a ritual at day's end before

a Santa Clara window watching the sun go
    over the Santa Cruz mountains into Pacific
waters rekindling closeness to her ancestors'

journey and a link with her husband my father
    who often drove us to Brooklyn's Hudson harbor
at sunset so I bow before her Light always in my life . . .

HOMAGE TO MY FATHER

"THE TIME OF THE BIRDS"
by Edwin Cook (1915-1966)

Yesterday following shopping at bargain town near Kennedy airport, I drove back to Flatbush through Rockaway and stopped at (you guessed it) Riis Park Beach. Mom stayed in the car, since it was so cold, while I walked alongside the ocean.

I never saw so many species and number of sea gulls. Each beach at the water's edge was literally covered with birds eating clams and mussels that were washed up on shore. The birds rose in swarms as I approached close to walk among them. I called as to a friend, but they were afraid. Only when I stood still did they remain close. I could understand cries of anger and defiance that I had disturbed their domain. I felt as if an interloper, which I was there at this time of year. Let's call it the time of the birds. So I respected their wishes and left.

(from my father's letter, when I was in the convent)

II. THE BODY POLITIC

A CALL TO "THE COMMONS"

divinity's concentrated *Be-ing* pours into our imperfect
   earthy dwellings designing destiny's playful mixtures
of you me we they us stirring every one's intergalactic

   chemical combinations spinning DNA's amazing auras
constellating a marvelous *falling in love with all* affinity
   under sun moon stars drawing down and up pulsating

yin-yang energy orbiting within/without nurturing calm
   dispelling fear reconciling antagonisms healing
hurts fostering harmony bringing down barriers tossing

aside *know it all* attitudes refusing to scapegoat others
   releasing high pressured expectations for perfection
recalling how *saving face* matters to most so going gets

gentle conjuring currents of kindness accepting flaws
   yet offering shelter from storms seeking to understand
even if not understood listening outside familiar circles

standing side by side with whoever wishes us nearby in
   the letting go of comparisons working as a community
cultivating compassion in the communal garden of our

hearts' kinship with plants birds animals moon sea stars
   planets human/divine beings as if we're learning how
to be whirling dervishes dancing together at dawn and dusk

23

CHINESE MEDICINE AND THE BODY POLITIC

thankfully Taoist philosophy filters through Chinese
medicine's centuries old healing practice with herbs

and acupuncture though it's true we in the West often
resist responsibility for our attitudes prone to project

blame outside ourselves for unhappiness including
illness at times taking a prideful position refusing

to listen or learn from those holding opposite views
a merry-go-round spinning conflicts at quite a clip

projecting wars at home and abroad deepening
duality's divide casting so-called enemies aside

while Taoism teaches subtle steady hidden healing
via the body/soul's natural flow waiting in the wings

for us westerners to awake/erase either/or letting
Life little by little happily rebalance through helpful

herbs and a practitioner's wisdom releasing deeply
embedded sites of cold/heat fire/water above/below

our unique universal home grown temple so peaceful
pin-pricks release hard held stubborn obstacles as we

learn a slow sure surrendering so static harmful stuff
cruises away up/down around/about harmonizing

relationships in welcoming the East's age-old wisdom
with their gifts of healing help for our wounded worlds

BENEFIT OF THE DOUBT

innocent until proven guilty, given benefit of doubt,
    offering rehabilitation, after all who is without faults,
taken wrong turns, though often successful folks
    boast as if their wonderful works in the world are
examples every one "should" emulate, forgetting
    humility goes a long way towards building bridges
to those we fail understand, what good does it do
    digging in our heels, dissolving dialogue, flinging
mud at another's motives, presuming bad intentions,
    forgetting religious founders called their followers
to love every one without exception, no matter slander's
    slap, some brave souls shall dare speak boldly outside
the box, though too often sadly suffer the consequences

INNOCENT EVEN IF SOMEWHAT GUILTY

innocent until proven guilty, benefit of doubt,
    haven't we all at one time or another jumped
to conclusions, condemned someone we don't
    understand, labeled others selfish, bigoted,
while ignoring empathy's practical daily challenge
    even as we preach diversity, yet may simply
forget the prophet's call to care for all, none
    excluded, challenged to seek lost sheep, welcome
any prodigal home, forgive seventy times seven
    and more, sprinkle mercy as Easter's holy water
everywhere even though tis true: easier loving
    only those who love us, honestly hard as heck
being kind to someone who may hate us, yet you,
    me, we, they are only human after all is said
and done, besides haven't you/I been judged
    unjustly at times, no self-defense, a perennial
challenge rises ringing bells for a story of a wedding
    where every one on the street was invited into
the feast while water was happily changed into wine . . .

OVID'S EXILE

such amazing courage by Ovid after Caesar's cruel
    banishing the poet to an obscure Black Sea town
far from wife, family and home in Rome, so lacking
    any affirmations, he continued composing through
freezing frosts, scorching summers, only to die after
    many years in exile without loved ones near; thus
my challenges are tiny compared to Ovid's bravery,
    yet speaking honestly: isolation by anyone in the arts
is far from easy, trying to keep faith in future readers,
    blest by the kindness of family, friends and strangers,
especially helpful if isolated during a pandemic, such
    a blessing arrived via a poet-friend offering his skills
as a proofreader in the nick of time towards this work's
    chaotic completion, while on behalf of all poets I send
bouquets of gratitude backwards over time to brave
    brilliant Ovid who continued composing incomparable
poems during the harshest exile until he died doing so . . .

STANDING SIDE BY SIDE

Isn't every one bestowed at birth with an instinctive
    empathy for all, hopefully encouraged as a child,
eventually coupled with free choice challenges,
    existential calls: give or withhold compassion,
act heroic or cowardly; not knowing in advance
    who will tap us on the shoulder, maybe someone
standing for things we can't stand, stereotypical
    scapegoat, we may jump to conclusions, project
prejudices, fail ponder our flaws, since "a better
    than thou" attitude's unconsciously endemic to
early, mid and present America, told vividly in
    Hawthorne's "Scarlet Letter" as townsfolks rallied
round the respectable gentleman-minister who

26

turned his back on the woman he seduced, causing
   Hester Prynne's condemnation, no public or private
   self-defense permitted, thus this perennial Puritanical
attitude permeates our country's collective/personal
   psyche casting labels over those considered less wise,
less noble or kind, while negative labels are tossed
   around, a powerful majority deciding another's fate
unfairly, thus Hester forced to wear a red "A" on her
   dress, similar witch hunts portrayed in Arthur Miller's
   "The Crucible" re: Senator McCarthy's 1950's pursuit
   of political conformist litmus test testimony of purity:
"Are you, or anyone you know, now or ever before been
   a member of the Communist Party?" A hysteria still
floating through American history, Freud designating
   such "the super-ego's better than thou syndrome,"
powerfully promoted by mass media, spilling over
   among friends, families, acquaintances, especially
if someone expresses a view other than the dominant
   "wisdom," risking scorn, lectures, put-downs, fear
of losing one's job, staying quiet even if disagreeing,
   thus kept in check by subtle censorship, overt or
implied, canceled, fired, not hired, stigmatized, such
   a silent self-censorship may permeate any society

HOMELESS IN CALIFORNIA

1.

one hot August afternoon, my grandkids
   saw someone curled up on the sidewalk
bundled in layers of clothes by a grocery
   store in our California town. I whispered:
"Sorry to wake you. Are you okay?"…"Sure.
   I was going to wake soon anyway."… "Hi, I'm
Carolyn. These are my grandkids, Madeline and

27

Ethan."…"Pleased to meet you. I'm Geraldine
but I like being called Gerry."…"Can we bring you
    a cold drink?"…"Sure. That would be nice."
The kids run in the store, saying: "Let's get Gerry
    a large lemon-aid drink and a cheese sandwich with
lettuce and tomato."…"Such a nice surprise. I'll save
    my sandwich till later."…"Will you accept some
cash?"…"Thanks, please put it in my purse. After
    the stroke it's hard to hold things. See my hand is
twisted."… "There's a Catholic Worker hospitality
    house in nearby San Bruno by El Camino. They
serve meals and offer shelter."…"Oh, I grew up
    Catholic. Maybe I'll go some other day." After
dropping the kids at their parents, I'm home
    in Pacifica and find the address for the Catholic
Worker intending to give it to Gerry next time,
    only I never saw her again. Was she chased
away from the store, as happens in most Bay
    Area cities. I feel regret for not driving back
to her that day, or for offering to take her there . . .

                    2.

a young man appears bewildered as he stands
at the corner of Bush and Van Ness Avenue in
                    San Francisco
                    this Sunday,
dark circles under his eyes, I'm close enough to
notice through a café window as I sip tea and
                    enjoy pizza from
                    nearby Whole Foods,
where my car is parked at California and Franklin,
suddenly he disappears, likely heading towards
                    the lush public park
                    in Pacific Heights

28

home to several wealthy politicians, so it's rare
to see homeless folks in this neighborhood unlike
            the Tenderloin;
            such a panorama
from the park's summit: Angel Island, Alcatraz
Golden Gate Bridge, Sausalito, Mount Tamalpais
            and gleaming east
            plush Berkeley hills
unlike the lowlands of west Oakland, where poorer
folks live, since segregation's a subtle stark reality
            in northern California
            where tech companies
flourish without doing much to alleviate poverty
failing to offer work opportunities and training
            for disadvantaged
            young people to learn
even entry level skills, though these world-wide
successful companies proclaim liberal slogans
            but do little if
            anything actually
to make a difference for disadvantaged folks, instead
play a part perpetuating discrimination by denying
            work opportunities
            for poor people,
as this young man who is likely unemployed and
searching for a meal at this moment, shouldn't I
            have stopped writing,
            put away poetry,
rushed outside, offered help before he vanished,
since I knew few soup kitchens open on Sundays,
            did I assuage
            my guilty conscience
by giving a dollar to a homeless man by 280 before
driving back to my lovely Pacifica home, mortgage
            paid, no debts thanks
            to my late husband's

job in academia, though I've made zero as a poet,
unlike those teaching in academic institutions, but
                that's veering off the path
                of facing the homeless,
who appear unexpectedly in least likely locations
as crucial reminders of the abysmal disparity in
                America between rich
                and poor, whom we
primarily ignore unless it makes us feel good to
protest injustices since afterwards we head back
                to our segregated
                neighborhoods,
schools, work-places, perhaps proud of publicly
letting others know how social justice conscious
                we are gladly
                offering cash,
a meager gesture considering the hugely radical
economic educational societal changes needed . . .

                        3.

nowadays, given a world-wide pandemic people
seem upset over the homeless at risk for Covid-19
                as if suddenly in
                California a crisis
looms for our most vulnerable, guess we've forgotten
that panhandling is forbidden by law in Palo Alto
                so if someone starts
                hanging out on any street
and appears to be down and out, they're not allowed
to linger by the glitzy Apple Store and fancy eateries
                where the well-to-do folks
                gather on University Avenue
within walking distance of Stanford, *suddenly* it seems
we progressives are shocked by the living conditions
                among the homeless

30

and nursing home elders,
while both populations have been neglected for decades
and sad to say not simply a federal problem, after all
this is the wealthy
State of California
sheltering super rich high tech firms, who stash profits
abroad, pay minimum taxes, if at all, off-shoring almost
all manufacturing
jobs, so why do I say
such things, perhaps as a poet wanting to make a dent
in hypocrisy and hopefully change things for the better . . .

HOMAGE TO PROTESTERS
in memory of Rosalie Rienzo

once upon a time Botticelli stood in the shadows
watching Savonarola burn at the stake for heresy,
fearing a similar fate, he destroyed his paintings
of non-canonical Greek mythical figures, less he
be condemned as a heretic, a self-censorship
for fear of losing his life, similarly though different
parallels as artists and activists face hard choices
as David Cornwell's author alias John le Carré to
prevent governmental crack-down lest his works
be condemned drawn from years as an MI-5 agent;
add to the list Daniel Ellsberg, Chelsea Manning,
Edward Snowden, Julian Assange, Glenn Greenwald,
Laura Poitras risking jail by releasing governmental
cables exposing U.S.'s surveillance of us citizens plus
apparent war crimes by American military against
prisoners abroad, while here at home in Oakland,
California I recall Rosalie Rienzo's public protests
confronting the Catholic church's male hierarchical
discrimination against women in denying equal
access to the priesthood, she stood on the cathedral

steps after Mass and asked the bishop why he failed
support women's ordination, this she dared do under
    the threat of excommunication, persisting till her last
days, a beacon of bravery beside past, present, future
    protesters advocating for religious, cultural, economic,
educational, political equality and social-justice actions . . .

RESISTER: ROY BOURGEOIS M.M.

a plea to pray for Father Roy Bourgeois whose
devotion to the oppressed in Latin America by
    founding the School of the America's protest
movement against U.S. military training of death-
    squads for Central America so Roy dared do
what many may only preach by his practice of
    crossing Fort Bennington's *"No trespassing"*
sign thus sentenced to jail-time though celebrated
    by the Church for this social-justice-peace work
yet swiftly condemned when he participated in
    a Mass con-celebrated with women so punished
by the Vatican in banishing Roy from the priesthood
    plus exile from his life-long religious community
while Wikipedia's list of the Excommunicated
    now includes with Joan of Arc Roy Bourgeois

IN MEMORY OF JAMES FOLEY (1973-2014)

In 2014 American journalist James Foley was
    beheaded by ISIS in Syria. In prison he used
his knuckles to pray the mysteries of the Rosary.

A graduate of Marquette University, a social-justice
    progressive Jesuit institution. Via a few media
outlets James's mother publicly decried the U.S.

government's failure to try and save her son. She
    was forbidden to raise funds for his release and
doubted if the administration's words were true:

"The United States never pays ransom money for
    kidnappings." Recently in my notebook from
a Marquette Political Science class emphasizing

where conflicts will arise in the future: Iraq, Iran,
    Lebanon, Egypt, Libya, Yemen and Syria! Would
my life be significantly different if I had pursued

teaching in International Relations and not veered
    into Political philosophy which led me via Hegel
into poetry! Few poets change political realities,

though Daniel Berrigan, Denise Levertov and Galway
    Kinnell raised awareness of harmful deeds done by
America at home and abroad, as James Foley risked

his life reporting about atrocities in dangerous places.
    Once captured in Libya, then released, a respite at
home, soon volunteering to report on Syria's civil war.

I berate myself beside other liberals/progressives
    for not protesting against our popular Democratic
president and administration's failure to intervene

for James's rescue, while continuing weapon sales
    to ally Saudi Arabia's military actions in Yemen's
civil war. Such is the perpetual sense of America's

entitlement/enlightenment, illusion/delusion, hubris
    at the start: Salem witch hunts, McCarthy/Hoover's
communist crusade, on-going Cold War with Russia.

33

Enough already as we say in Brooklyn! Did I/we speak
   out, do anything on behalf of James Foley? Where was
I when in 2014 as his mother pleaded for her son's life.

Mea culpa, mea culpa, mea maxima culpa. I pray Christ's
   Mother with angels welcomed James Foley into heavenly
paradise that he believed in while praying the rosary R.I.P.

PALMYRA, SYRIA

At a distance via a few photos on tv ISIS is seen
   erasing the Syrian people's past by destroying
                Palmyra's Temple
                of Baalshamin,
blasting this 2000 year old sacred site of worship
   where countless people offered incense, flowers,
                while carrying in
                their sick for healing,
leaving the ashes of loved ones in alcoves, calling on
   ancestral spirits in rituals, a people who've endured
                droughts, desert storms,
                earthquakes, fierce conflicts
over centuries, their temple walls surviving threats,
   perpetually until now: 2015 such a shocking sight:
                Palmyra crumbles as
                casualty of a prolonged
war aided and abetted by foreign powers, as U.S.A.
   with Saudi Arabia fighting through proxies to gain
                hegemony against Iran,
                Russia and Bashar Assad,
head of Syria, so in the chaos ISIS strafes Palmyra with
   machine-guns, bombings, defacing, defaming this
                site to smithereens,

killing people seeking
safety in crumbling shelters, as the director of Palmyra's
ancient antiquities, Khaled al-Asaad, is tortured since
he refuses to disclose
where precious artifacts
are hidden, a silence costing him his life, as a U.S. news brief
mentions his head displayed on a pillar of the destroyed
temple he tried save,
while we in America
went along our merry way as if nothing was happening
on the other side of the world where our money helped
fund this war by
offering military advisers,
ignoring how Saudi Arabia and Turkey allowed ISIS to
pass through their lands to fight in this Syrian civil war,
while the U.S. continually
preached to Europeans
they should welcome asylum seekers, as if we had
nothing to do with this tragedy, so refugees pay
smugglers for passage
to reach Europe, or if
without funds, they slip into run-down Turkish camps,
though Germany's Angela Merkel publicly pledges
to welcome 800,000 refugees,
England offers 20,000 a haven,
France 24,000, and the U.S. 25,000 over four years!
while we're a major funder of this war sending
4 billion dollars in military
equipment and training,
by following Bush in destabilizing the Middle East
with invading Iraq, executing Saddam Hussein,
suppressing U.S.'s role
supplying nerve gas
to Iraq for its war against Iran, though peace activists

35

petition President Obama to take in refugees, few
        public demonstrations
        before the While House,
not wanting to offend or criticize a liberal administration,
        that at the start failed to face international accusations
        of war crimes by Bush,
        Cheney and Rumsfeld,
a placating message: "Let's not look back, but ahead,"
        thus the perennial U.S. refusal to take responsibility
        for harming other
        countries' people,
forget restitution, instead perpetuating the myth of
        American exceptionalism proudly professed to all . . .

A PERENNIAL PEACE ACTIVIST
in memory of Pauline Thompson

Easter/Passover time a reminder of the late
        Pauline Thompson who every year during
Holy Week protested publicly at UC's Lawrence
        Livermore Lab against their link to nuclear
weapons research so she gathered with a group
        crossing the prohibited line though struggling
with her walker when past 80 obvious in a news
        photo showing police escorting Pauline into
a van with others for overnight in the crowded
        county jail abuzz with young activists perhaps
she reflected on ravages she witnessed as a nurse
        in France during WWII followed by becoming
a Quaker practicing non-violence along with
        her rugged northwest upbringing staying active
into her early 90's the most prolific in a creative
        writing class I led where she shared doses of

36

wit honesty kindness and a pioneering feminism
      forged for decades with a childlike pleasure
alongside serious studies in psychology through
      San Francisco's Jung Institute and Analytical
Psychology Club where I blessedly met Pauline

ON THE ONE HAND OR THE OTHER

Is it possible to become even briefly an impartial
      spectator seeing several possibilities before swiftly
banishing opposition rather make room for diverse
      opinions look simultaneous at several viewpoints
discover common ground singularity/multiplicity
      embedded in everything spiritual human high low
in-between hidden manifest animal mineral daring
      to toss out the window dogmatic rigid rules no longer
insist only one way should suit all instead consider:
      Hegel's thesis : anti-thesis=synthesis and Aquinas'
life work responding to theological problems as posed
      with several respectful summaries of each one with
his beautiful prose so isn't easy to discern which he
      preferred over another all seemingly valued then at
the end he confided to a confidant: "All my writings
      are as straw compared to God's Transcendent love . . ."

ARTIST/ACTIVIST, W.B. YEATS/MAUDE GONNE

Sun through fog, waves crashing along Sligo's
      western coast, where Yeats often walked seeking
communion with spirits above/below in clouds
      and cliffs, so decades later, after he passed, people
wondered if the woman he loved saved his letters
      and poems; tempted to toss them into the bin;
no matter since throughout his life her presence

37

stayed, sometimes disguised in poetry as a wild
wonderous woman muse embodying Ireland's
    legendary beauty; this woman whom he adored,
proposing marriage, feeling the blow of No; instead
    she chose a well-known political activist as partner-
husband, not the dreamy poet, yet she outlasts time
    in his lines, stanzas indelibly embedded with signs
of their being lovers side by side on a Sligo bed in
    the eternally green glory of an Irish summer . . .

ART AS A POLITICAL ACT
in memory of Penelope Etnier Dinsmore

. . . that afternoon sunlight was shimmering
    in the cove below us while willows were
clinging to cliffs as herons swayed in a nest
    atop a pine overlooking the Pacific coast
while you said this is where you walked daily
    with your beloved dog Seri then we paused
below a Douglas fir to touch lacy green lichen
    waving in the wind while sounds of waves
rose and fell as you spoke of when a girl diving
    off your father's boat along the Connecticut shore
at night floating on your back seeing scintillas of
    stars and felt without words they were somehow
divine messengers then at your grandmother's home
    when you were sleeping on an enclosed porch
one summer seeing magical lights of tiny winged
    creatures on the screen so in the future you'd paint
golden lights on canvas with a childlike sense
    of wonder as you express wishes you had done
this or that in parenting though justly proud of
    your adult children simply admitting the challenge
was not easy as mother and artist calling for double
    devotion these things you said simply and I replied:

"Bravo" for your accomplishing both beautifully but
    ever modest even shy in an unassuming way you
dismissed my compliments so it's happened that
    you've passed over and more than ever I treasure
our conversations discussing divinity's disguises
    in dreams Nature art family love loss life's
twists turns so I've saved your farewell message
    on the answering machine spoken with gentle
courage while I honor your presence in the golden
    painting you created now on the wall across from
where I write daily a personal universal testimony
    of the Divine permeating our entire lives . . .

AS LITTLE CHILDREN

forest creatures sanctuaries alcoves safe-places
    propagating laurels oaks pines firs maples
hawks owls woodpeckers finches bluebirds
    a chorus cleaning our climate correcting us
careless humans who continue emitting pollutants
    forgetting to beg Nature's pardon since driving
our cars claiming it's the only way to get around
    quickly or whatever our excuse we affluent ones
keep up frequent flying except during a pandemic
    but let's celebrate less meat eating as a turning
towards a more humane way of treating animals
    as we move closer to a plant based diet while
trying to act again as children laughing at twigs
    stuck in our hair brambles tickling our legs
trees waving hello taking time to bow our thanks
    standing again awestruck at a storm running
again through summer fields rolling down hills
    singing to a pet hugging our loved ones up close

TRAIL BLAZER HANS KÜNG

Hans Küng's teachings via Vatican II Council liberated
　thousands through his promoting "the priesthood
of the people" emphasizing equality, empowering
　every one to think and act more freely and though
Küng stayed a priest he continued teaching and writing
　progressive theology at Tübingen University then
after John XXIII's death conservative popes reasserted
　papal rigidity regarding no way would women be
allowed to become priests will liberal Pope Francis
　open ordination equity thus far the Vatican's silent . . .

POPE GREGORY'S LOVE FOR TRAJAN

only one pope prayed publicly for the soul
　of a deceased emperor that being Gregory
for Trajan and in doing so defied church
　teaching that anyone born prior to Christ
was too late for heavenly salvation thus
　the soul trapped forever in Limbo a fate
Gregory refused to accept as final instead
　convinced that Trajan's good deeds far
surpassed most Christian rulers certainly
　deserving a blessed reward which Gregory
prayed for daily perhaps under the Arch of
　Trajan itself with the inscription in Latin
"Pontifex Maximus" a title taken over by
subsequent popes throughout the centuries

DARING TO DREAM AFTER DEPARTURE
　in memory of Joseph Grassi

the warm September air was rising in the field
　where he was walking along the road coming

40

from the seminary to celebrate Mass at the convent
   while I was meditating by the window watching
his tall slender figure and knew well of his brilliant
   down to earth insights in sacred scripture plus
talk of a deeply compassionate nature and obviously
   an innovative liturgist while I was an inexperienced
untamed unconscious young woman keen for love
   eager to offer everything more personal than a call
to missionary work abroad for a ten year stretch such
   musing now decades later recalling the apple orchard
sweet smelling pink clusters on silvery branches scenting
   the air as I walked with my sisters to work for the men's
wing of our community so sensed a synchronicity of
   spirit and sensuality in the Spring air foretelling good
times ahead asking for our leap of faith into a shared
   future we two as one converging we heard the Dove-
Spirit's call to face the future together in trusting Love's
   blessed times ahead birthing two beautiful children

ODE TO SENIORS AND GRANDKIDS
for my grandchildren, Madeline and Ethan

Leaving off snacks at my grandkids' home today
   a chance to wave at a physical distance, say Hi
gaze and guess how each one is doing, act as a kid
   myself which always happens when with them,
until the pandemic closed schools and prevented
   us seniors from intermingling with young folks,
a loss felt by thousands, maybe millions, though
   lucky me living 10 minutes away by car so I try
seeing the kids even if briefly once a week: "Here
   I am in my mask from Mars!" doing a goofy dance
before asking how they are, then waving goodbye,
   while later I walked around their middle school,
standing on grass under trees familiar from days
   I met the kids after the bell rang, when M. asked

41

"Can we stop at Starbucks?" before driving her home
    or to her Dad's classroom, E. saying he wanted to
walk with a buddy and meet me later, sometimes
    M. saying she'll go with friends downtown too,
like her brother, whatever, no problem, though now
    this Saturday I stand solo beside dear familiar trees
by their empty school recalling times past waiting
    with other grandparents in those uncomplicated
lovely days when we took such joys for granted . . .

ODE FOR AN OAK

Unfortunately things do not always turn out as we wish
As now across the globe people are suffering from a virus

Yet surprises do pop up as during a hike along Millbrae's
Crystal Springs trail suddenly I see as if for the first time

A magnificent ancient oak who I've been passing by not
Noticing till now such astonishing beauty so I promised to

Compose an ode for this precious being whose roots solid
In earth send strong branches swaying twigs to tree top

Under a bright blue California sky as breezes stir debris
Rising from the ground pushed by winds off the reservoir

While clouds coast in strong currents over the ridge from
Nearby ocean a picture I long to hold as a locket clasped

To my heart so at home trying pay homage to this creature
Of great beauty though after hours of work I pressed

The wrong key and it all vanished as a dream along with
My vain hope to post it on FB for some Likes thus perhaps

A punishment for pride yet again I'm composing an ode
In homage to this oak praying thanks in humble adoration

Reminding me some things are meant only for the soul's
Intimacy not for public sharing yet this attempt simply

Arises to praise laughter woven with lichen twigs hanging
On gnarled graceful indescribably beautiful symmetry

Likened to a complex symphony intricate architecture
Of a cathedral confounding words best beheld by birds

MAMA CAT'S PURRING

I hear her little heart in humming
purrs as paws rhythmically knead
   a blanket while golden tipped ears
twitch happily as black/white stripes
   ripple along her entire body tail
waving "yes" close to ecstasy after
   being rescued from an aggressive
raccoon who tore her fur now safe
   from harm not holding grudges
for my rescuing her later not sooner
   she's simply the soul of forgiveness
licking my hand as a loving friend she
   persists since perhaps she feels I am
her Mama sitting close in a sunny circle
   on the couch while winds howl outside

THE ASSUMPTION'S POWERFUL PROCLAMATION

the terra cotta wall in Chartres cathedral's crypt
   glows with a faded mural of the great mother
and child in this once upon a time site of worship

rivaling the Trinity to some theologians' dismay so
they commissioned Thomas Aquinas's *Summa* as
a way to reassure such primacy seemingly strange

nowadays though tis true liberal Vatican II council
downplayed devotion to Mary with the excuse of
not wanting to alienate ecumenical possibilities with

Protestant denominations that might be turned off by
imagined superstitious Catholic rituals as candle
lighting at shrines in her honor yet remarkably noted

psychiatrist Carl Jung publicly praised the Church's
proclamation of Mary's Assumption to Heaven as
the first time in history such a significantly symbolic

act possesses power to change all aspects of spiritual
political cultural psychological religious economic
ways the world will now feel pressure to reconsider

women's rights in rebalancing relationships regulations
thinking acting within the male institutional world
which Jung believed needed feminine integration . . .

KIDS AT HEART

laurels pines manzanitas oaks sequoias
fostering a fresh Spring chorus calling us
careless humans to quit polluting the world
drive less fly infrequently ride bikes walk
hike regularly boycott inhumane factory farms
harming helpless animals before becoming
food for our tables sorry if I sound gross am
preaching to myself as well affluent among
privileged folk compared to my grandparents'
generation now here I am with a garden of

lavender rosemary thyme azaleas geraniums
   forget-me-nots lilies palms roses jasmine
irises abundantly blest by butterflies bees birds
   forests wild flowers ocean shores inviting me
to see again as a child open to wonder laughing
   as twigs stick in my hair fur and cobwebs cling
to my clothes if I dare climb a tree fun coasting
   in memory's sled down snowy slopes in a local
park tumbling together in a heap jumping head
   over heels into a summer lake riding a surf board
dancing to music under the stars in a school yard
   awestruck at a full moon's high tides approaching
the once in 800 year affinity Jupiter and Saturn felt
   in up close conjunction brushing past each other's
orbit *oh ah* as grandpa always shouted at the July 4th
Coney Island fireworks magical mystical call it
what you will within the stone circle ancestors
   praying for dawn's first light acting again as if
elves fairies druids angels sprites owls lambs
   kids running home with friends before night falls
lying on the living room floor coloring with crayons
   sketching our adventures the young teaching us
grown-ups how to thrive on God's green earth . . .

THOMAS AQUINAS   (1225-1274)

1.

. . . he struggled in solitude year after year
   composing the Summa Theologica, that I
studied at age 19 in the convent novitiate,
   a ponderous inaccessible boring treatise,
at least to me, till recently I read a paperback
   edition, surprisingly thrilled by his presenting
opposite views so seamlessly I can't figure which
   opinion is his or someone else's since every single
summary shows positive points evoking sympathy

as Aquinas explained each ethical, philosophical,
theological perspective as lots of pieces completing
    a harmonious whole puzzle, perhaps consciously
practicing compassion for various valid pathways,
    without disdain, discovering good intentions in all

2.

nowadays who cares a fig about Aquinas,
considered by many as obscure, not worth
    reading, best left to gather dust on library
shelves, rarely taught except in traditional
    seminaries, yet his influence circulates in
residues of faith felt by a few, including me,
    though I conceal my attraction to him from
friends now daring to admit in a poem . . .
    secretly loving how he weaves opposites
into beautifully composed complex conclusions,
    distilling disagreements, creating tinctures
of insight, slight-of-hand magical potions, plus
    potent doses adding lustra to our lives if we
read his puzzling solutions poised perhaps to
    seduce readers of dull theological tracts with
surprising generously outpouring of sympathetic
    analysis on every page, simply refreshing tonics
to put us asleep with sugar plums dancing in
    our dreams, angels spinning on pin-heads . . .

3.

Aquinas hibernates in my memory of a deceased
    Jesuit Ted Mackin who spontaneously loved to
quote by heart the one he thought *a sage* in speaking
    of human nature, politics, ethics, relationships,
not in a superior way, simply sharing something
    that mattered to him with friends, since Aquinas's
Summa permeated his life practically after years
    of study at Rome's Gregorian where his works

were taught; then for decades Ted taught Canon
Law at Santa Clara University, where in his later
years he launched a new life, leaving the priesthood
to marry, who can say if the *Summa* played a part
in highlighting all walks of life as equally valuable . . .

4.

. . . now I evoke your writing in trying to stay
faithful to the One you adored by following a call
of composing Divine Presence in earthy prose as
your life's goal presenting pros and cons, opposites
balanced side by side, relations rubbing shoulders
in summaries, each placed beautifully on the page,
respectful of disagreements without put-downs,
even if beliefs differed from yours, kind magician-
mage with your compositions, refusing to reveal
your preference, not seeking fame, instead keeper
of the flamed Spirit Dove divine, scattering the
"I"/"me" equation out of the picture, letting ego
go, then traveling to Santa Fossanova Abbey,
you were knocked off your horse by a branch, close
to death, confessing to a confidant: "my writings
are as straw compared with Love's Transcendence"

DIVINITY IN ONE AND ALL

It's hard for us humans to see sparks of divinity
struggling within every one since easier dividing
the so called good from what is often thought
the evil ones we label self-centered and worse perhaps
a Freudian unconscious pleasure tossed in the mix
of feeling we and our friends groups etcetera are
more enlightened easier to pounce even politely
toss reconciliation aside bypass self-examination
of our conscience instead get a high if pointing to
faults of "those others" so cancel close down dialogue

prevent possible reconciliation or healings all around
having forgotten the long ago prophet's plea to seek
lost sheep and warmly welcome every one home . . .

HEALING DEEPENING DIVISIONS

who said it's easy following the prophet's call
    to love enemies as we love our friends or self
for that matter simple enough offer excuses
    resist listening to the other side especially in
politically polarized times though be prepared
    if you dare say something in defense of a view
other than the popular one you may be verbally
    attacked especially if expressing empathy for
folks opposed by supposed enlightened noble
    ones who may actually look down on anyone
outside their circle of consensus calling others
    bigots not worth talking to yet do you dare
defend the hated ones knowing the risk of being
    cut off in discussions silenced preached to by
those who believe they're caring and you're wrong
    in listening to multiple views instead they may
proudly parade their beliefs and good deeds front
    and center or on public pedestals for emulation
forget modesty or shyness and so it goes arrows
    of hatred hitting hard is it better to stay silent
yet aren't we all imperfectly flawed needing
    compassion why not try fostering dialogue
even if labeled by friends as sympathetic to
    supposedly selfish ignorant stupid people
so suffer cold shoulders since the popular folks'
    view may forget we are all fallible humans
who may suffer secretly at times make serious
    mistakes seek compassion need forgiveness
as lost sheep needing a warm welcoming shelter

PRISONS, PARDONS, PURGATORY

I'm on a quest seeking signs of mercy in stories,
   history, religions, politics, while I sip tea in
a San Francisco cafe, once again shocked at
   such a fateful punishment for Satan and his
fallen angel followers, as portrayed in Milton's
   Paradise Lost, where they grieve in Hell
for the loss of a once beloved heavenly home,
   such a harsh punishment for a single act of
rebellion leading to devastating consequences,
   shocks me, yet compassion's possible for
repentant humans who dared disobey God's
   ethics, thus Purgatory's purging in hope
for an eventual paradisal bliss and since we
   never know who is cast in eternal fires, even
though Dante decided he did, I feel grateful for
   belief in repentance up to the moment of death,
brings pardon through a temporary punishing
   place, so the Catholic practice calls us to pray
for all deceased, thus offering a second chance at
   a happy afterlife, though taking time depending
on misdeeds or sins of omission, this in-between
   purgatorial place as prelude to Paradise, sooner
than later with prayers in the present for deceased
   ancestors, strangers, friends, relatives, whoever
needs a helping hand boost, if only transgressions
   were wiped away as well in our U.S. penal code,
where rehabilitation remains a low priority, instead
   severe penalties are perpetuated to poor people,
who can't afford a top-notch defense lawyer to fight
   for their rights, sadly true even in liberal California
when "three strikes against the law and you're in for life,"
   no pardon possible, a perpetual hellish sentence,
hope for change by a proposition ballot down the road . . .

SAUL/PAUL

super zealous Saul constantly chased followers
   of that renegade Christ fellow whom he hated
so drew his followers into a dragnet of persecution
   with an over the top self-righteous confidence
ruling the roost among colleagues friends family
   till one day riding his high horse on the road to
Damascus Saul is suddenly knocked down by
   lightning and a thunderous voice shouting:
"Saul, why are you persecuting me?" "Who are
   you?" "I'm Christ you attack in my friends."
So shocked to the core, pleading for forgiveness,
   granted a pardon and given a new name "Paul,"
apostle to outsiders, no longer part of an exclusive
   enlightened elite, now facing fresh criticism for
befriending Greeks, Romans, Assyrians etcetera

RANDOM KINDNESS

   I've tried to keep faith with the Pentecostal
"good news" of the Holy Dove's multiplying
   presence in tongues and disguises even
 daring to imagine kinship with bluebirds in
   the forest of our souls surprised coming
upon Christian ancestors Pan dancing at
   a bend in the road Demeter descending
in fields of sunflowers Daphne's sheltering
   laurel grove a redwood tree waving above
the fog a family of feral felines purring indoors
   teaching me thanks for rescuing little lives
endangered by coyotes and yes I confess having
   taken wrong turns goofed become a public
scandal tried not hurt others while being true
   to oneself not so simple so I learned subject
to rumors swirling behind my back deserved

or not a small price to pay for kinship felt
with women who were publicly condemned
    besides blest beyond belief I've clung to an
ancient faith bestowed in Brooklyn beginnings
    where I witnessed acts of random kindness
healing hurts lots of laughter rubbing shoulders
    daily with all around good will among friends
and strangers every day no matter circumstances

ODE TO HOSPICE VOLUNTEERS
for Nancy Newman

Oh let me sing praise for an angel of mercy
    who for over 20 years has tended to those
on the threshold of passing over offering
    her patients courage and comfort to face
whatever awaits relieving anxiety easing
    pain through her Reiki practice laying
comforting calm hands over the patient
    the way Christ did ages ago though
she is contemporary beautiful smart
    witty which people enjoy as she gives
hours of care with a humble heart having
    experienced Life's profound challenges
so let's raise our voices offer a toast in
    thanksgiving for San Jose, California's
Nancy and all hospice workers as they
    stand as sentinels of compassion devoted
to the sick and dying while comforting
    families with caring support and courage

ROME, AFTER CROSSING THE RUBICON

After crossing the Rubicon he returned triumphant
    to Rome, a man like a god, exalted above others,
evident as he marched across the Forum towards

51

the Senate. Applause. A clash of swords saluting
his arrival. Voices shouting: "Hail Caesar!" "Pontifex
Maximus" eventually inscribed at the entrance arch.

. . . as nearby incense simmered in the underground
enclosure of the Vestal Virgins, who were kept there
since childhood, like prisoners, assigned for life with
state duties to serve gods appointed by male priests
and rulers to preform on-going rites day and night for
so-called common good of the Roman empire . . .
. . . on the other side of the Palatine Hill is the shrine
to the Magna Mater, who over centuries some
say evolved to become the beloved Madonna caring
for the poor and persecuted, her mural portrayed
on catacomb walls beside shrines to her Son the young
Shepherd carrying lost and wounded sheep home.

NOVITIATE DAYS NEAR SALEM, MASSACHUSETTS

She loved hearing birds calling in the forest
during late October when the red ivy reached
high in the pines edging the novitiate boundary

poplars swaying a beautiful birch grove maples
aflame at sunset preparing for profession of
triple vows to the One she believed created it all

rainbows taken as a tangible divine enchantment
owl calls roses in a blooming Spring golden red
icons stamped on a Lady Slipper's pale petals

intricately woven spider webs glistening dew
in the corner of a side path on the way to chapel
wild wheat waving in a field where she hiked

with her sisters sharing dreams where they wished
to be missioned stories of growing up in various
places across the country relaxing in warm weather

overlooking a pond and the daily pleasure she felt
chanting psalms back and forth across the aisle in
Latin cadences strangely appealing on the tongue

sounds of starlings heading home she pulled back
curtains round the dorm bed moonlight on blanket
simple gifts yet not without underlying shadows

since this was near Salem where ages ago women
were executed as witches or driven into the wilderness
like the woods where she walked often with her sisters . . .

MOZART TO THE RESCUE, SAN FRANCISCO

today's dark clouds seemingly somber mood
    lift once we are engrossed in Mozart's "Magic
Flute" caught up in the trials of happy-go-lucky
    Papageno and Papagena singing alongside
more serious Tamino and Pamina who face scary
    forces forecast by a witch-like Queen of the Night
figure the two couples sing through unfamiliar
    mazes and challenges cheered on by a chorus
of children in the wings offering sweet courage
    sparkling hopeful notes gently fanning a theme
that things will turn out okay after twists and turns
    confusing signposts they will come through
a labyrinthian ordeal back to the beginning as
    we all hope happens for us as the curtain falls
we rise together applaud cheer the company
    some throw flowers on stage we walk hand
in hand down the opera house steps opposite

53

city hall's gleaming black and gold dome due
to recent rain then we take 101 south to our San Jose
    home seeing a full moon shimmering on the Bay
as we hum *pa pa pa pa pagena   pa pa pa pa pageno*

III. HOMAGES: PEOPLE, PLACES

PEOPLE

HOMAGE TO A MONASTIC WOMAN
for Sr. Veronique, Redwoods Abbey, California

Driving north on 101 for five hours from Marin,
we pass mustard fields, vineyards, towns, malls,

while listening/talking non-stop, since you're
returning from your sister's funeral in Belgium.

We're heading back to your monastery, where
I'll make a retreat while grieving my mother's

recent passing. Engrossed in our conversation,
I miss the exit for Garberville, so back track to

southern Humboldt county, causing late arrival
for community prayers, though no sweat since

you wink and smile mischievously across the aisle
as we bow singing the psalms. Not one to abide

strictly to The Rule, living the spirit intended, not
bound by the letter when choosing compassion,

laughing beside retreatants doing dishes, devoted
to all God's creatures, bringing a bouquet of wild

flowers to your "mother madrone" after Mass before
manual labor assignment. If only Thomas Merton's

wishes were a reality that contemplative communities
included families as full-time residential members.

Maybe Joe and I might have raised our kids within
this communal setting. Not permitted by the Vatican,

yet many of us rejoice that you and your sisters
warmly welcome all retreatants to this spiritual

environmentally sacred refuge among magnificent
redwoods and experience your mentoring example

in honoring Nature as Divine, no preaching, simply
authentic acts you practice of adoration to everything

inside and outside chapel, as when you brought me
to your favorite grove to pray, such radiant simplicity

in your face as you spoke: "The child within every one
needs loving care." You led in prayer lifting your

arms to a trio of redwoods encircling us. Then we
walked to chapel through a field of tall grasses as

a deer looked up from grazing by the forest's edge.
Our last time together, hard for me to leave. We

hugged, blew kisses before you headed to the kitchen
and I began driving 101 south towards Golden Gate

Bridge into San Francisco. Not a final farewell, since
you keep me company with notes, pressed leaves and

flowers from the field we walked, plus inspiring quotes
on cards, comforting through the passing of my beloved

husband. Ever reassuring prayers for my grandkids'
well-being, remembering details of their lives, faithful

friend through joys and sorrows, supporting my poetry.
I look forward to driving back to your welcoming arms.

HER DOWN-TO-EARTH DIVINE DEVOTION
for my sister-in-law Loretta Cook

Remembering the last visit to my brother Richie,
    who went through the mill of cancer treatments
and a stressful hospital stay, home at last where he
    wanted his wife Loretta's loving care. How well
they knew each other, high school sweethearts,
    having raised six children, now nine grandkids
living nearby. Always anticipating his needs: "How
    about your favorite sandwich for lunch?" "What
about that tea you like, or I'll brew fresh coffee."
    "Here's the remote so you choose what to watch."
Neither brags about good deeds they do for family,
    friends, community, strangers, church, whoever's
in need, they simply notice, respond over the years,
    preferring unsung practices to preaching, as now
clearly I see Loretta's devotion to Richie in illness,
    changing bed linens, providing clean clothes,
on-call night and day without complaint, a home-
    grown Brooklyn girl of loving Irish immigrant
parents, and until his sickness Richie and Loretta
    helped daily with the grandkids, who visit regularly
as she loves cooking for family, no FB, no texting or
    twitter, she stays in touch with relatives and friends
via the phone or in person, such an inner strength,

warmth, smartness, sense of humor, deep religious
faith (never spoken of since she dislikes self-promotion),
    caring in big and little ways for Richie's comfort,
reassuring him when it's time for a peaceful passing,
    which she made possible in gathering their three
sons and three daughters around his bed, holding
    hands, praying the Our Father, each one together
telling him: "We love you" and Richie's last words
    looking up at Loretta and family "I love you" . . .

CHINESE MEDICINE
for Dr. Efrem Korngold
Chinese Medicine Works, San Francisco

Resting on the treatment table as my pulse
    is checked by the acupuncturist who
discerns weaknesses needing silvery
    needles to set free the chi energy's
healing flow from feet up around down
    and up again under ultra-violet light
diminishing pain reviving little springs
    spiraling along the dark forest floor of
self so to release blockages thanks to key-
    meridians acting as clearing-sites for
natural paths the way chants rise/fall
    through the room's speakers playing
in the background as breezes blow back
    window-curtains at the corner of Noe
and 24th Avenues in San Francisco as I
    drift in day-dreams Pacific/Atlantic
memories/hopes past/present injuries
    /strengths lost/found faith/doubt
yes/no anger/patience old/young
    infinite/mortal sun/moon earth/sky
sickness/health sleep/dance yes/no

resist/join yin/yang multiple/singular
harmonizing differences centuries of
    Chinese wisdom healing us westerners

FELINE MENTOR SIMBA

Beautiful, sweet, strong, golden furred feline
    Simba has passed over, ever patient with
children playing, faithful comforter listening
    through your sensitive ears to a child's tears,
such an appreciative audience gently sitting
    as little Madeline sang songs, allowing her
kisses, stroking your tummy and when curled
    asleep opening eyes to let Ethan carry you
overhead to a feeding-station in the kitchen.
No hissing or claws drawn, only tempted to
run outside if the front door opened, eager to
    run wild outside, hide in hedges, brought back
for safety's sake due to traffic, only fault, if such
    it was: loud persistent meows for more food,
especially if you smelled turkey sandwiches I
    was making for the kids, a natural mentor
from the start teaching me trust in feeding you
    with a tiny baby bottle since as a kitten small
as a sparrow you fit in my palm, such sweet
    glances, purrs, serenely sleeping, alert in a flash,
blinking thanks, placing a soft padded paw on
    my hand, I compose this poem to thank and
honor your showing me ways for accepting
    whatever life brings while sprinkling mischief
just for fun in daily doses multiplying smiles,
    leaping laughs, dear beautiful feline being
may your sweet spirit spring into our lives
    when we need you the most! gracias Simba!

BLESSED BE THE BEES

1.

... growing up in Brooklyn, I'd run, sometimes
   scream if I heard a bee buzzing by a neighbor's
forsythia bush across the street from our apartment,
   though over the years living in California, I tried
practicing what I preached to our sons about staying
   calm when bees appear, try learn to trust they're
simply doing what comes natural propagating roses,
   lavender, lantana etc. busy being bees gathering
nectar while riding waves of pleasure till sundown
   beelining home as drones for their honey hive

2.

... what wonders bees might teach in classrooms
   or preach from pulpits, probably they'd avoid boring
do's and don'ts, instead simply spin songs inspiring
   communal quests for the good of all, these wise
miniaturized disguised divinities, a working choir,
   not requiring rehearsals, dispensing tonics, bypassing
pharmaceuticals, producing medicinal sweet amber
   liquid dark/light dosages, warmed if you wish in
tea or taken straight on a spoon, depending on taste
   or medical diagnosis, options open as a Japanese fan,
helping heal colds, headaches, restore vitality, while
   avoiding dogmas, spreading good-will via hexagon
havens serving as a metaphorical cooperative natural
   alternative to rigid so-called scientific or religious
orthodoxy, sharing their wonderful community's
   simple complex structures harmonizing beauty with
practicality as any magnificent cathedral's interior/
   exterior design does, ah if we could easily, without
being stung, peek inside the miniature mysterious

abodes of these furry yellow/black/striped beings,
after they've busily foraged in flowers, home-bound
   to a heavenly haven humming happy hymns as if
a choir from miniature stalls . . . praising their Queen

3.

German friends Chris and Wolfram share photos
   via the internet of building bee hives with their
sons and friends in readiness for a Berlin Spring,
   showing how after absence/presence as the way
is with grandparents who fly in from California
   celebrating together in the garden seeing fruits
and flowers multiplied and thanks to bee shelters,
   making possible an extended family's joy tasting
thick golden honey spread on bread & stirred in tea

FILOLI GARDENS, WOODSIDE, CALIFORNIA
for Mary Jeanne Oliva

the Filoli garden guide pointed us to "the Jesse Tree"
   though we searched in vain, so settled on a hedge
resembling Chartres cathedral's window highlighting
                    Jesse's lineage,
                    opening a pathway
where we wondered aloud if it's possible to decipher
   our ancestral heritages as arranged in plants, bushes,
trees, while wandering within a labyrinth of lavender,
                    awestruck by a magnificent
                    redwood offering nooks
and crannies for countless creatures over centuries,
   food storing bins, nesting sites, way-stations as
with monarch butterflies heading south seasonally;
                    these we pondered
                    facing a glorious mimosa

grove along the mountain ridge where beeches swayed
below, yew trees attentively side by side reminding
MJ of her gifted gardener grandfather who taught her
how to recognize
lineages among trees,
this thought sent me down the trail recalling my husband
Joe's words about his Italian grandfather as an artisan
cabinet maker creating furniture from trees, while raising
veggies galore in their
Westchester garden,
leading MJ and me back and forth through aisles of foliage,
grateful for feeling personal family roots in Nature, so
she continues in cultivating her Santa Clara garden, soon
time for lunch,
eggplant sandwiches
in the café, then surveying further a few more paths we
especially loved lined with our new found friends
among maples, oaks, willows, yews, pines, magnolias,
lavender, verbena,
rosemary, parsley,
thyme, lilies, marigolds, azaleas, roses, forget-me-nots, as
willows were waving while we walked to our cars, time
to hug goodbye the way friends do on such a splendid day

HOMAGE TO DR. SHERMAN WONG, SAN FRANCISCO VETERINARIAN

. . . after taking in feral felines, I needed a veterinarian;
so through a Cat Rescue Network, I located Lynn L.
who opened her small Oakland apartment for cats labeled

unadoptable. She said: "Supposedly "No Kill Shelters"
do not exist, since if a cat fails their entrance test for
adoption, the rescuer must pick up the rejected cat by

24 hours, or the animal is put to sleep, only trainable
    ones are welcome." Lynn, disabled in a wheelchair,
surviving on social security, her works and words were

inspiring, as she added: "No cat is hopeless. Given loving
    care, all cats can learn to trust. Go to Dr. Wong, the best
veterinarian in the Bay Area!" So I began bringing

rescued cats to his healing hands, then one day Fuzzy
    secretly ran away, not being outside since rescued
three years ago; scary, since this is an open space area

with coyotes, raccoons, bobcats; so morning, noon
    and night, I searched nearby neighborhoods, calling
"Fuzzy!" shaking a jar of his favorite food, leaving

treats on the patio, tell-tale signs of a raccoon next day,
    dirty paws in empty bowl, while I worried if Fuzzy
was dying of thirst, since a severe California drought,

no water nearby, then three weeks after vanishing came
    4th of July fireworks, sparklers, rockets, cherry bombs
past midnight; if Fuzzy was close, he'd have fled, some

friends said I should accept no return, yet after lighting
    a candle by Francis Assisi shrine, I heard a growl by
the patio from a golden furred feline cowering close,

tuna fish lured him inside, so the next day Dr. Wong's
    gentle strong hands over frightened Fuzzy: "Please,
tell us how you survived for three weeks? Your ears,

eyes, mouth, teeth are fine. No scratches, though dried
    worn paw pads, not surprising as you've probably
traveled far from home. Heart and lungs are strong.

Let's see you walk, good. Now the scale, such a big boy.
   No need for blood test. You're good to go!" An exam
as fine physicians offer human patients, primary care,

surgery, specialist caring for various species of animals,
   providing a peaceful end for the terminally ill, offering
comfort for grief-stricken care-givers, adoption advice;

ethical, never unnecessary tests or treatments, mentoring
   veterinarians, pro-bono practice for pets belonging to
poor folks, Dr. Wong, SF hero, 3 cheers! Meows! Woofs!

HOMAGE TO ROBERT BLY AND NAOMI CLARK
in memory of Naomi Clark, founder of San Jose Poetry Center

Memories ripple in clouds along the coastline of
my mind listening to Robert Bly reciting Yeats's
poetry by heart at the San Jose Poetry Center,
when he first came west thanks to Naomi Clark,

offering a weekend writing workshop at her Santa
Cruz mountain home, he asked participants to go
outside and choose something in Nature, then write
about it as if a detailed dialogue whether with a plant,

leaf, rock, feather, fruit whatever; while I was lingering
along a trail overlooking the ocean, Robert walked by
then stopped, so I dared ask: "What do you think of
wanting to write political poems?" Smiling he said:

"Always write whatever you wish. Feel free to choose
a topic. Compose without fear of censorship by anyone,
including yourself. No critic on your shoulder." Then
suddenly he said: "I love seeing your soul in your eyes."

Such a surprising compliment, no one ever said such
a thing, so I've held his kind words in the honey-hive
of my heart for possible bleak times, plus his prophecy:
"An earthquake's simmering within your stanzas."

Soon my life turned upside down, split in the middle,
I was cast adrift, so sought Yeats's poetry as first heard
recited by Robert when he came to California at the start
of his career thanks to Naomi's bringing him west; yes,

she helped countless poets, me too, by sending a poem
of mine to a journal, an acceptance boosted my confidence
and she invited me to read at the poetry center; I celebrate
kind, talented, generous poet Naomi, who died too young . . .

IN MEMORY OF JAMES MERRILL

Daring to phone, I was surprised by your warm
invitation: "Do come over for tea." Such a magical
afternoon, your saying: "Love is like religion in

its devotion to another" since I lamented "Up till
now, my life has been smooth sailing" "Well, we
wouldn't really want it to be smooth sailing?"

Staying silent, thinking: I prefer a calm lake to
a stormy sea. We talked of life's ups/downs,
joys/sorrows, you said: "grist for the mill of life

and poetry." Your photo as a boy knight in a play
displayed on the piano by your grandmother
as these rooms used to be her home. "Well, you

will take more tea, won't you? No need to rush
off. Besides, here comes Peter who will join us."
My camera framed you as a loving couple. In

saying goodbye I asked: "Is it ok if I write you?"
"Why, of course, and I'll write as often as possible."
"Should I call you Jimmy?" "I prefer James. My

mother calls me James." A five year correspondence
sprinkled with your sweet witty casual candor,
comments about life, friendship, your Stonington

garden, plus honest self-disclosures and sage advice.
I was unaware of your AIDS diagnosis, though re-
reading your letters, mortality is mentioned several

times as at my dear pet's passing, you kindly replied:
"I still feel the fur of my long deceased Massie rubbing
round my ankles on many a morning when I open

the refrigerator. How wonderful, if at our passing,
the Bach cantata is played: "Bist du bei mir" whether
addressed to God or a beloved person. It says every-

thing I could hope for at the end. "If you are beside
me, I will go joyfully to my final rest." And that is
surely the comfort you were able to give your ancient

companion." It happened you passed over during
vacation with Peter in Arizona. A generous gesture
of friendship in a Valentine's card with your phone #

arrived while you were staying there. I planned
phoning for your birthday. Too late since you died
a few days prior due to complications from AIDS.

Months later the doorbell rang on a rainy day in
San Jose, priority mail delivery of your posthumous:
"A Scattering of Salts, Poems by James Merrill"

with a note from your publisher that I was among
a list of friends you wished to receive your book.
Large damp circles stained the cover as if heaven

was weeping. I wondered if the title related to
Stendhal's book on the stages of love akin to tossing
a branch in a salt mine only to discover on pulling

it out, tis covered in crystals. Your thank you note
saying for years you intended to read this book. Who
knows if influential in the title of your beautiful poems.

A MAVERICK JUNGIAN
in memory of James Yandell M.D.

Jungian therapist/writer warning against dangers
    of any powerful "collective group" pressing for
conformity, playing the trickster role at gatherings
    if certain views were placed on a pedestal, he'd
upset the popular narrative by questions, turning
    things this way or that, suggesting fresh views,
raising doubts, defending anyone scapegoated by
    others, always turning the tables with wit while
blazing new trails in Jungian psychology above all
    by befriending the "shadow" as a focus in funny,
smart, brash, brilliant prose and presentations, not
    shy to publicly and privately admit mistakes,
faithfully encouraging colleagues, patients, friends
    to feel at ease in owning their human limitations,
so led to liberating repressed emotions little by little,
    rather than suddenly exploding, possessor as well
of a gentle humility with a wry smile, he'd mention
    mischievous things he did thus throwing a wrench
at too pat and proud a position, helping others accept
    fallibility by his down to earth examples in releasing
one's shadow without harming others, so laboring in

the vineyard of psychology, mentoring, healing, writing,
presenting with full disclosure of limitations, ethically
   devoted son to his aging mother for decades, faithfully
caring for his daughters' welfare, rebalancing insights
   within his professional practice, readjusting his opinions,
kind friend for many, empathetic to the core, relating with
   every one respectfully, now missed by all who knew him . . .

NATURE'S MAGNIFICENT FELINES

Lucky, Blondie, Feathers, Gypsy, Galahad, Hermes, Iris,
Mama, Fuzzy, Fluffy, Simba, Nala, Bodhi, Moonie, Mika

twinkling golden eyes mischievously adventurous
   felines rippling soft fur sticking to my clothes
unassuming casual teachers loyal companions
   after years yet I'm still a novice at learning your
language of purrs meows hisses growls silent
   staring before springing across at string curled
in a closet crouching under a couch camouflaged
   behind curtains pristine irrepressible instincts
doing what comes naturally ears flatten signaling
   about to pounce perhaps at dust-balls better yet
if catnip a spider sister/brother/roommate quick
   recovery calm composure forgiven no grudges
fast as a flash for food bowl contentedly followed
   by grooming self or generously for your sister or
brother occasionally humans included in licking
   my fingers no apologies for not working feverishly
at any jobs doing what comes naturally is enough
   a chore (unless a feral seeking prey for food) all
felines frequent nappers dreaming noises twitchers
   perhaps traveling to kittenhood wild teenage years
romantic relationships rough and tumble escapades
   near death self-defense experiences facing coyotes
pouncing just for fun sighs snores paws kneading

blankets claws spread happily if gently petted safely
home sudden waking yawns long yoga-like stretches
   resting forehead to feet on paws or around another
friendly feline synchronized breathing as I stroke soft
   fur behind silky ears under-chin furry tummy as tail's
happy fluttering cat smile in sleep whiskers twitching

ARTISANS OF OLD

anonymous artisans who built cathedrals without
   carving their names in the facade, opposite to many
moderns prizing personal prestige as a goal seeking
   praise, rewards, glittering etcetera stuff associated
with acclaim/fame, such a contrast with past painters,
   stone-masons, architects, glass cutters and others who
contributed complementary skills to create vaults, steeples,
   buttresses, sanctuaries, altars, labyrinths, portraying
saints, sinners, angels, demons, gargoyles, while laboring
   in sweltering summers, freezing winters, fading Autumns,
flowering Springs, few named, each one's work worthy
   as every one else as a team shaping magnificent sites of
refuge for people to gather, share their loves, losses, joys
   and sorrows, alleluia thanks to anonymous artisans
setting an example for every one today tomorrow raising
   families, driving trucks, trains, buses, teaching, healing,
offering catharsis in the arts, office workers, high/low
   tech laborers, countless individuals and together serving
in hospitals, shops, schools, theaters, offices, homes, crucial
   individually/together linking lives today to laborers of old
. . . who built for their Creator a better more beautiful world

VERDI'S ERNANI

the vacant December field's golden haze
glistens in memories of summer's spent stems
   as pines stretch tip tops into a darkening sky,
the sun's sinking goodbye rays west into Pacific
   waves while Verdi's Ernani/Elvira duet reaches
every inch inside my car as I recall a farewell
   when someone I loved stood at a doorway where
the country road curved past rows of forget-me-nots
   though when in driving coast highway with the CD
playing I kept my hands on the steering wheel
   recalling how I was unable to wave goodbye to
a beloved forest fading in a rented car's rear-view
   mirror farewell to trees who witnessed my heart's
hopes errors losses mistakes set in the month of
   March happenstance same season different year
by decades when my father died later called by
   a counselor "an ungrieved grief" though long ago
my ignorance almost overruled my Capricorn's
   practical nature helping bring me back though
before leaving I faced Long Island's cliffs rippling
   over the shimmering Sound this time listening
to Verdi's lovers pleading for mercy and pardon
   to the one with power to save their lives instead
a stern unbending retribution in a crescendo of
   "No! No! No!" as the judge turns his back on
calls for forgiveness reminding me on first seeing
   hearing this opera in San Francisco overcome
with sympathy for the couple's desperate plight as
   they beg for compassion instead were met with
a resounding revenge which failed to stop their
   cadences of tender love as they leaned into Verdi's
powerful heart-breaking tidal musical lines falling/
   rising in resurrections sailing across the ages . . .

JOHN DONNE (1572-1631)

dear realist, sensualist, poet, skeptic Donne
   rolled into one until broken-hearted by loss
of your best beloved's death, you turned to
   a religious haven in your heart while also
serving priest-rector of Saint Paul's cathedral,
   delivering sermons, ministering to the sick
and dying, presiding at baptisms, weddings,
   funerals, while daily faithful to your call as
a poet trying to integrate life's complex passions
   into lessons for letting go yet honoring love's
sensual unashamed appeal over years of longing
   and knowing magnificent wonderful affection
with a partner who died too young, you continued
   writing while trying to weave human and divine
love in serving formally as a priest by preaching
   and practical care for a community, surely at
times bouts of loneliness amid struggles and joys
   that you placed before God in prayerful poems

SUNRISE WITH YOU IN VENICE
in memory of Joseph Grassi

You were walking towards me over an arched bridge,
   sun rising behind your head and even at a distance
you possessed an aura of optimism, that no adversity
   could extinguish, even though your mother died so
young. You survived years of rigorous religious training,
   inheriting a tough endurance thanks to your Italian
father's immigrant example of hard work at an early age.
   Your eyes blazed with fiery gentle rays, intelligence plus
a child-like simplicity and love of Nature. Even decades
   later, as you approached death's door, your equilibrium
steady, living naturally, you'd say: "Today is the best day
   of my life." Memories' comforting courage as when

across the Grand Canal we entered the cathedral, standing
    together awed by Titian's Assumption of the Madonna
highlighting life's sacred, communal, personal, un-nameable,
    inexplicable blessings in every season, then hand in hand
we walked over the foot bridges back to Piazza San Marco
    passing the plaque honoring John XXIII, once pastor here,
we bowed in thanks for his Vatican II Council liberating us
    to marry, so celebrating our wedding anniversary in this
country of your ancestors, enjoying wine and bread, we
    hummed along with gondoliers singing *O Sole Mio* . . .

HOLY YEAR PRACTICE

an old Catholic belief in Purgatory as a temporary
    purifying place forgiving crimes/misdemeanors/
transgressions transforming souls into a healing
    happiness, set free for flying to paradise thanks
to in-sync happenings on earth as the Holy Year
    ritual calling all parishioners to go on pilgrimage
to various churches as a way of helping release
    the deceased stuck as if prisoners in purgatory
seeking help from living folks praying to lighten
    their sentences unfortunately twisted in prior
times when money for indulgences was practiced
    by the church leading to Luther's public protests
since he believed once deceased a soul was saved
    or damned no in-between possibility unlike
Catholics' faith that at the last minute if a person
    asks for forgiveness they can enter paradise though
may spend time first purging offences as a penance
    satisfying justice before sailing to heavenly shores
a system of equal opportunity for a happy afterlife
    so as a child I enjoyed joining pilgrims lighting
candles in three Brooklyn churches to set souls free
    via prayers though I'm aware modern folks call

such beliefs silly superstitions though the story's
    told of Shakespeare praying publicly by his son
Hamnet's gravesite shocking some present to wonder
    whether he held Catholic sympathies so risk possible
persecution or even death his famed works likely played
    a role in saving him from such fate thankfully over time
tolerance prevails for various religious practices even if
    sceptics wink at or scorn folks following beliefs that they
can make a difference by offering prayers for the deceased
    relative or not friend or stranger lovingly remembered

EDEN

when September's maples were slowly turning
    towards golden flames fanning the forest tiny
trumpets sounded leafy bushes tickled my legs
    then thunder rumbled far out to sea lightning
flashed in dark clouds yet in spite of all the signs
    some suggested calm conclusions while up-close
hugs and kisses hinted at the day's departing end
    as owls called over bending birches pines waved
hickories creaked on the roof swans in flight
    signs of winter's impending hibernation settling
down of creatures the hill's high nests emptying
    furry companions burrowing close in fallen leaves
heart-breaking silent sighs farewell among those
    species migrating summer plants stored indoors
hints gestures words signaling an ending farewell
    at a bus stop and the looking back one last time
sighting a beloved landscape over my shoulder
    beyond loss embedded forever memories' haven
a particular forest's scent sound flavor feel vision
    via a gift given a temporary visa into paradise

MIDDLE SCHOOL MENTOR
for Bertha Rodriguez

I'm typing poems at Peet's Cafe in Millbrae,
  California listening to Chinese, Spanish,
Arabic, Hindi, and English spoken all around,
  a multi-lingual town offering me a chance
to practice speaking Spanish whenever I pick
  up my grandkids after school, since Bertha,
the crossing-monitor, patiently helps me recover
  this language I loved and studied in college
ages ago, actually she mentors in more than
  Español. We share joys and challenges, plus
she offers practical smart kind advice if I ask.
  When my car wouldn't restart, Bertha calmly
coached me to try this and that, so following her
  instructions, I pressed a switch and presto
the motor started. My *muchas gracias* is for all
  she does during the school year for the kids,
their parents, grandparents, whoever crosses
  her path, ever smiling. *"Cómo estás Carolyn?"*
If something difficult faces me, I'm comfortable
  confiding in her compassionate practical heart.
An anecdote: I gave her a copy of my book "Heart
  and Soul." Her sincere *"Gracias,"* then days of silence
till I dared ask how she felt about the poems, saying
  most people don't like poetry, so it's ok. She replied:
"I don't know how to tell you this, Carolyn, but
  someone stole your book off the ledge here, while
I was doing my job helping the kids cross the streets.
  When ready to go home I couldn't find your book.
So sorry." I was laughing: "No problema. Whoever
  took it will be surprised! Poetry's not worth much
money." During the pandemic, Bertha was not working,
  though recently she has returned as school reopens
with her wise caring ways to guide us at the crosswalk.

ODE TO NATURE'S ARTIST
in memory of Penelope Etnier Dinsmore

faithful friend of Inverness's Point Reyes forest
  hiking trails daily beside your dear rescued dog
Seri welcoming light/shadows/darkness Nature's
  messenger weaving night and day dreams with
shapes colors presences on canvass following
  a call felt in childhood discerning divinity's link
with birds sea sky trees flora fauna all creatures
  near and far working devotedly through decades
to make the Spirit visible on earth while bringing us
  all closer mediator of Jungian insights loyal strong
for family and friends beloved by David in the home
  he built as an architect for your art complementary
couple honoring solitudes coming together every
  evening around the table overlooking Tomales Bay
sharing wine dinner candles music Seri close by

A MINISTER'S LABOR IN THE VINEYARD
for Rev. Vance Eckstrom PhD

thanks to the internet I found a former colleague of
my late husband Joseph, Vance Eckstrom, who moved
years ago with wife Clarice back to their home state
of Kansas. Now I'm reading his dissertation with

a surprising note: "You are the first person to read it
since acceptance by the graduate committee." I hope
my response will make a difference in knowing his
work was appreciated. Though like my own thesis,

it may continue sleeping on the shelf, unread, till
who knows when? Whatever its fate, I'm happy to
have his work in hand and see how it opened an
opportunity for teaching at a Catholic university,

rare at the time for a Protestant theologian, which
is how our paths crossed since my husband Joseph
worked for diversity in the university's Religious
Studies department that he chaired, so hired Vance,

who received high praise by students for six years,
strongly recommended for tenure, though turned
down without reasons. Was Vance ahead of the times
emphasizing ecumenism when sectarianism existed.

We joined friends helping Vance and Clarice pack for
their move back to Lindsborg, Kansas, where he taught
at a university, while serving as a Lutheran pastor.
Now decades later this chance to read his dissertation

on Karl Rahner's Catholic theology as being compatible
with Protestantism; proof Vance was a prophetic bridge-
builder teacher, underappreciated years ago, though
nowadays such ecumenical approaches are expected.

Retired in his 80's, voluntarily driving miles to serve
needy rural communities, who need a minister's
comfort and courage; this I only learned by asking:
"Vance, what do you enjoy doing on weekends?"

A FRIEND AT HADRIAN'S WALL
in memory of Fred Tollini S.J.

a photo you sent me shows your radiant smile
    as you lean against Hadrian's wall in northern
Britain under a clear sky with clouds gathering in
    the distance over rolling hills behind your head
while flocks of sheep feed by fences facing town
    during a weekend break while you're teaching
Shakespeare at Durham University for Santa Clara
    University's summer program such a joyful

expression in your gaze who knows if for a special
     reason since strict Canonical rules keep tabs
on your vocation definitely marriage not an option
     best not get too close to women and yet far from
home were the Roman soldiers sent centuries ago
     to this outpost opposite to Italy's warm climate
though true your community allows vacation choices
     ah this lovely location perhaps enjoyed warmly
with the person taking this photo no scandal just
     friendship or were you harboring hopes for a future
suggested by Shakespeare's *As You Like It* actually
     what would happen would be your recommitment
to the path pledged long ago in your native California

IN MEMORY OF HUSTON SMITH

Unforgettable joy driving you to a favorite
Berkeley Chinese restaurant for lunch rice
     carrots green beans plus a bowl of noodles
while time seemingly stood still as I gazed at
     child-like eyes of wonder and your glorious
smile whatever the topic but always you'd first
     ask directly about whatever personal concerns
I shared at our last meeting such an incredible
     caring memory we flowed easily between what
mattered most at the time family writing books
     world religions soon the hour and a half flew by
so you'd say: "Let's see who picks up the phone
     first for our next time." then unexpectedly in 2007
we faced different yet similar difficult challenges
     yet managed to meet not at your home this time
I came to your Assisted Living Residence room
     opening the door such a radiant welcome with
wide open arms so bending down for a hug you
     drew me close as I heard your sobbing words:
"I'm so sorry what has happened to you." (the only

other time I saw a man cry was my brother on
the night our father died) we prayed together
   then I drove us to your favorite restaurant when
you said: "Well, Carolyn, we both are living in ways
   we did not choose, but I'm convinced we will come
through." that thankfully happened as you returned
   home cared for by your wife and a Tibetan couple
until you passed over before we met again no time
   for a final farewell yet your presence remains when
I recall your kind words and compassionate ways . . .

CARAVAGGIO AND HIS CHRIST

once upon a time centuries ago a group gathered
   in a darkened room arguing over money matters
when suddenly a stranger stood in the doorway

pointing to Matthew who was collecting the taxes
   and on looking up he fell in love at first sight
with the one they called Christ so immediately

left everything to follow him in this biblical story
   painted by Caravaggio that draws people to
ponder Christ's outreach to someone looked down

upon by many supposedly fine people yet like
   a magnet this "Why me?" glance of Matthew
may have comforted the painter in the process

since he would be continually pursued by police
   as a criminal in fear of capture so hide in towns
far from his home till he decided to sail back

to Rome and boarded a ship that stopped at a port
   where suddenly he fell seriously ill and missed
the call for "All aboard!" waking too late he ran

after the ship dizzy from fever falling on hot sand
    seeing it disappear in the distance he collapsed
delirious near death's door did his beautiful Christ

appear as in the painting of Matthew this time
    looking in Caravaggio's eyes calling his name
holding him close carrying him home to paradise

HOMAGE TO DOMESTIC WORKERS

. . . once upon a time I was a member
    of a community where we were trained
as social workers, teachers, doctors, nurses
    to serve poor marginalized people in Latin
America, Africa, Asia, though not all were
    missioned, some stayed stateside as
myself assigned to count money donations
    for the missions directed by the men's
branch of the Order, while several sisters
    labored in kitchens and secretarial positions
their entire lives, yet hoping for a mission
    assignment abroad, which was celebrated by
a bell-ringing ceremony as the congregation
    lined the road waving goodbye at the gate
with New Year's Eve noisemakers for sisters
    taking a taxi to the train for travel, air or sea
to distant countries, while other sisters stayed
    working in offices, kitchens, laundries; perhaps
creating a kinship bond with all domestic workers . . .

MEDITATION MENTOR
in memory of Judy Sullivan

After lunch free time for study, letter writing,
   laundry, meditation, walks in the woods before
classes. Such a surprise, Sister Rose inviting me
   for a hike. After all, we weren't close friends.
I hardly knew her. She arrived at our motherhouse
   from the Valley Park, Missouri novitiate, while I spent
those years training on the East coast. Sister Formation
   Year brought both groups together: college classes,
spiritual tune-up workshops before being missioned
   to Latin America, Africa, Asia or a clerical job where
I'd land next year assigned to count donations, in charge
   of bank deposits for the Maryknoll Fathers. Now this
warm Spring day pushing open the heavy door below
   words carved in stone: "Peace to all who enter. Grace
to all who leave." "How about heading up Cloister Hill?"
   "Sure" said I. At that time convent rules were easing
thanks to Vatican II encouraging personal growth work-
   shops. Gone strict guidelines as: "No talking in twos,
unless with a superior's permission." Banishing the fear
   of supposedly "particular friendships." Halfway up
the hill, she veered to the side, "Let's sit under that oak
   and just BE." What did she mean: "Just BE?" I tried
relaxing in the silence watching wildflowers in the field,
   while to the west golden Palisades cliffs gleamed above
the Hudson flowing past New York into welcoming
   Atlantic waves. Sure meditation was part and parcel
of our convent life, centered around gospel stories of
   Christ, while this was simply sitting silent in Nature,
without directives or suggestions. The bell rang for class.
   We walked back in a comfortable close silence. That
afternoon remains indelibly marked in my soul, echoed
   into the future, as when in a Los Altos, California zendo
I sat alongside a serenely silent community with a Shensi

whose wise simplicity inspired, as with Sister Rose's way
of "just being" close to God and each other under an oak tree

HOMAGE TO A FRIENDSHIP
in memory of Eileen Moore Sorensen

I pressed my back against the earth, feeling the tall
  wild wheat bend and thought how much I missed
my friend recently sent to the missions for 10 years,
  though I hid these thoughts from my sisters as
I gazed across the apple orchard. Though I shared
  my feelings of loss to her in my letters, while
preaching to myself that love ought to outlast any
  separation, even if we were never to meet again.
A turn in events when my superior called me on
  the carpet for things I wrote to my friend, making
it obvious that my incoming-outgoing letters were
  being scrutinized. So I gave up the freedom to write
as I wished and gave in to self-censorship, not that
  what I wrote was awful, but somethings upset
my superior. That was a long time ago and thanks
  to Vatican II strict religious community rules eased
as those regarding such things as the feared label of
  a "particular friendship." Yet an unconscious fear
or scar remains, a hesitation to write without self-
  censorship; thus I pray for pardon if anything in
this book upsets you, dear reader, not my intention . . .

HOMAGE TO A POETRY PATRON
for Mary O'Connor

  . . . your affirmations sustain my poetry's
  past present future flying down California's
coast between our homes the way ages ago you
  first planted seeded words of encouragement
for my poems as an experienced gardener which

81

you were for years a crucial part at the start
showering sunshine praise as needed plus doses
    of encouraging responses as energy boosters
I've carried composing like composting to grow
    confident when the going gets rough which is
inevitable over time now let me pause to celebrate
    your years as an outstanding social worker in
Hawaii then Peru where you met your future
    husband Jim settling down out west raising
a fantastic daughter serving as a counselor to
    Stanford staff till retiring to Sebastopol together
transforming an apple orchard into a flourishing
    grape vineyard producing the award winning
"O'Connor Pinot Noir" now widowed you continue
    nurturing family friends grandkids enjoying book
groups garden clubs bridge partners community
    concerns political causes sustaining arts as poetry

HOMAGE TO A REMARKABLE WOMAN
for Betty Adam Steidel

Sister Maria Fatima welcomed me with a radiant
    reassuring smile on behalf of the community that
I wished to join my feeling shy overwhelmed having
    traveled by subway from Flatbush to New York's
Grand Central Station then train along the Hudson
    for Ossining cab to Sunset Hill so Sister's warm
welcome eased my anxiety about the interview ahead
    with an elder serious sister in charge of accepting
admission to the community I was advised to wait
a year following high school which I did so joined
up at age eighteen never meeting Sister Maria Fatima
    again till my husband Joe and I moved our family
to California eventually Betty left after several years
    as a missioner among the poor in Peru where she met
her future husband Jim Steidel then they moved to

the Bay Area raising a fine family along with her
devotion for over 35 years to Saint Anthony's parish
    caring for the Hispanic community where she writes
the Sunday bulletin in Spanish oversees outreach for
    the dining room feeding hundreds organizes a major
Christmas toy drive for kids guides the catechetical
    teachers lovingly cares for family friends community
my Alleluia day when she opened that convent door . . .

HOMAGE TO A SAN MATEO COUPLE
for Pat and Jerry Motto

six months after Jerry died, you shared a photo
    where, newly married, you're walking side by
side as an elegant couple along a Viennese street,

he handsome, you gorgeous, your coats blown
    open in a summer breeze at the beginning,
just before you were married, followed by over

forty years devoted to family, friends, works
    in the community, he a Unitarian, you close
to social-justice causes since roots formed as

a Maryknoll missioner in Peru, no pressure either
    way to follow same path, freely flourishing,
his brilliance in psychiatry, plus practical wisdom

shared if a friend asked advice, his listening heart,
    not shy in discussions, honest, forthright, which
was appreciated, hands on helping at household

chores, fantastic couple's warm hospitality; now
    sadly you're sorting through his papers, books,
what to save, savor, recycle, give away, touching
what he held, reading what he read, noticing details

in articles he underlined, discovering letters from
grateful patients with thanks for saving their lives,

photos of family, friends, his growing up in Santa
  Barbara, serving in the U.S. Army during WW II,
driving supply trucks near the Battle of the Bulge,

liberating Nazi death camps, personally heart-breaking
  since his Jewish ancestors, so having witnessed war,
he chose psychiatry as a profession specializing in

preventing suicides, creating a letter-writing program
  for survivors as a way to save their lives, while the heart
of life was your love sustaining all that mattered to him . . .

HOMAGE TO FREUD'S *CIVILIZATION AND ITS DISCONTENTS*

Eventually I found Freud's final book helpful regarding
Love/life directives. As a physician of the psyche, he
  lobbied in his writings for individual freedom from
the do and don't rules imposed by subtle strong authorities
  within and without oneself, his encouraging liberation
in the let's not be so hard on yourself attitude by accepting
  limitations, feeling freer in letting go of pressures to
conform to idealized goals pressed on us by family, politics,
  friends, society, religion . . . He was moved by people's
suffering, so tried healing help via accepting human nature
  as flawed and needing compassion, not piling on more
Do this, Do that; instead he wrote how a dose of humility
  can temper so-called enlightened ones from self-righteously
harming other humans by their edicts, which he felt were
  forms of aggression and what Freud called satisfying
a narcissistic feeling of being better than imagined selfish
  "others." Such a short powerful last book is his passionate
call to ease suffering imposed by the superego self/society

causing deeply lasting damage. Not naïve about "the real
   world," as he narrowly escaped the Holocaust by fleeing
to England while suffering from cancer at the end of his life

RUSSIAN RIVER REDWOODS
in memory of my mother, Betty Ball Cook

This redwood trail overlooks the Russian River
   Valley's vineyards aglow in midafternoon as
the fog has lifted while I'm recalling my mother's
   passing over a few months ago if only she was
with me marveling at this pinesap aroma since she
   loved spraying perfume whenever we strolled
through San Jose's Macy's cosmetic department
   soon a gray-blue sky reveals birds in formation
as an arrow migrating south for wintering in Mexico
   I'm slowly taking the trail circling back by ancient
ferns alongside long ago fallen redwood giants of
   this forest softened humus path under my feet
signs indicating types of plants species of trees
   wonderful details of the width height and age
of still standing redwoods visited by countless folks
   then I reach the parking lot and turn for a loving
farewell to a magical magnificent mystical old-growth
   redwood pardon superlatives but she deserves such
praise when waving in highest branches as if in kinship
   with my mother's departed spirit then swiftly out
of the blue close to clouds a bird swoops down so
   I see and feel glorious feathers almost touch my face

PLACES

I AIX-EN-PROVENCE

The train chugged up hills round ravines, orange
groves gleaming in a bright August afternoon,

we registered at a hotel once a convent with its
cloister-like grille framing the front desk, an old
   confessional housed the public phone booth,
an angel hovered around a corner alcove, lunch
   outdoors along Boulevard Cours Mirabeau, we
toured a once flourishing monastery retaining
   an inner herbal garden, Saint-Séverin serving
as the local parish, red lamp glowing in shadows
   by the sanctuary, signifying eternal sacramental
presence, at the exit/entrance a mural of a phoenix
   feeding young from her heart near a statue of
the Black Madonna where we lit candles in thanks-
   giving for this our Wedding anniversary, then
the winding tram to Saint-Victoire's legendary land
   where Magdalene supposedly retreated after sailing
the Mediterranean from Palestine, her relics remain
   in the cave we visited, this site for a passionate
duet in Verdi's "Trovatore," how lovely our dinner
   by musical waters of a shell-shaped fountain, back
at the hotel-convent we celebrated love's divinely
   human marvels as moonlight illuminated our bed . . .

II PARIS FANTASY, SAINT-GERMAIN-DES-PRÉS

a summer night's warm air rising from the pavement
   as the gate opened to Saint-Germain-des-Prés park
chestnut tree shadows lingered on the shoulders of
   Apollinaire's statue footsteps on gravel music
seeping seductively from the café across the square
   true she fell foolishly for someone showering warm
words in that Left Bank garden while candles blazed
   continually inside at altars in this once-upon-a-time
abbey now a local parish church where she prayed
   to resurrect belief in grace's availability no matter
the transgression forgiveness at the core yes after all
   she admitted wrongs shamed for sure Life moved

on leaving glorious moments embedded in mistakes
　　she found the path as the gate opened the way grace
appeared out of the blue　a second chance after facing
　　flaws　begging pardon　having transgressed among
lots of lost sheep yet daringly grateful for falls called
　　Life lessons learned the hard way　profoundly grateful
while sheepishly smiling as she recalled the gargoyles

III　STRASBOURG, CROISSANTS

My first time in France since Joe was giving
　　a presentation at the Catholic Biblical meeting
in Strasbourg　each morning I made a beeline
　　for the bakery beside the cathedral whose bells
were ringing though I continued on like a heathen
　　seeking sustenance from sweet earthy savories
so stood in line like other devotees awestruck at
　　mysterious magnificent pastries on display
along the counter　such shapely crescent moons
　　called croissants reclining in blond-flaked gowns
wearing buttery slips concealing inner surprises
　　bitter chocolate　almond slivers　savory cheese
under puffy crystalline shimmering glazed surfaces
　　sprinkled with an angelic-like veneer of powdery
sugar　such a heavenly earthy breakfast presented
　　by artisan-like-priest pastry chefs　whatever gender
ministering to anyone with or without faith　fulfilling
　　more than hunger offering delightfully divine sweet
savory guilt-free concoctions even if eating two at
　　a time　no need for confession since impossible to
harm others on pastries though centuries ago gluttony
　　classified as a sin　no worries now to delight in one
more without qualifying for punishing ledger　though
　　gaining too much weight or above average saturated
fat not good for anyone though I confess a proclivity

to believe pastries may prefigure a taste of paradise
on earth better than Eden's plainly forbidden fruit
    besides here all are welcomed with or without faith
in spiritual matters simply desire to consume and rejoice
    in deliciously beautiful baked concoctions composed
with a holy aura hovering over their appearance akin
    to statues of saints in church alcoves though these
seemingly miraculous creations are thank God for
    tasting here and now reasonably priced let's lick
our lips hum alleluias as available at bakeries back
    home too offering similar earthy/divine delights . . .

IV PARIS, ONCE UPON A SUMMER

remember the green bench by an open gateway
    with a little park beside Saint-Germain-des-Prés
where trees were sparkling with sunset and across
    the square a mime was stock-still then suddenly
started break-dancing as a tapestry of moon and stars
    lit the scene during our first night in Paris and who
knows for sure if an illusion or "real presence" akin
    to priestly powers of words transforming bread
and wine into Christ's body and blood not meaning
    anything sacrilegious only that everything in sight
seemed charged with God's down-to-earth grandeur
    as food fashion faces cafés shops flowers trees
transformed by a luminous aura of ever-lasting beauty
    the way it was as a child hiking with other city girls
to a Catskill mountain top where we stayed overnight
    in a cave till dawn rose round Mount Zorn sending
shafts of light into Silver Lake as dreams mingled with
    the steaming sunny serene scene of mists suggesting
a sacred ritual akin to Holy Communion as I struggle
    for words in homage to magical moments engraved
in memory no matter the source simply seen felt sacred
    forever as it was as well in Paris that summer . . .

V AVEBURY'S STONE CIRCLE

we were walking within Avebury's sarsen stone
   circle set in place millennia ago seeking warmth
during a harsh winter touching these turquoise-gray
   beings who seemed to be watching as we came
close to their silvery streams and steaming crevices
   revealing rainbows of tiny magical pools after
recent storms helping us to let go of thinking we
   know many more things than these supposedly
inert stones who are capable of being silent teachers
   standing in as metaphors for life's rough surfaces
made smooth by surrender to sequence of seasons
   in a patient attitude awaiting solstice recycling as
reunions happen among friends families communities
   near and far none excluded a doing what comes
naturally akin to how children show us the way
   the world was at the start and is eternally young
in this place built cooperatively by hands in humble
   rituals honoring earth and sky's sacred relationship
so we join the welcome round the bend singing Alleluias

VI VENICE

since you never knew how the taste of honey
   melting in tea that day led to her appreciating
yet not replying to your letter impossible to explain
   simply say transcendence played a role limitations
embraced love and forgiveness rising from ashes
   defeat folded into insights mixing compassion for
oneself learning a lesson after all who are we/they in
   the end middle or at the start readily condemning
anyone without knowing the before during and after
   state of their heart and soul yes you made love in
that magical inexhaustible place for poetry painting
   architecture religion music food fiction film add to

the list if you've been there surely know well what I
   mean such an inexhaustible source for passions and
excuses of every sort rising from the breath of boats
   waterways lovers artists artisans musicians cooks
opera aficionados why shouldn't certain scenes go
   a long way towards redeeming whatever scandals
plague us humans fragile foolish fallible beings we
   all are yet be again with me beside the proud tower
by the Bridge of Sighs as a gondolier's serenade echoes
   in channels while rowing the couple who lean against
each other on cushions in the graceful black gold-trimmed
   boat as burnt sienna walls of the Moorish-designed Ducal
palace windows gleam with the sun's intricately intimate
   allure mixing with San Marco's earthen-baked simplicity
creating a fierce casual atmospheric tension as turquoise
   touches sea and sky simultaneously rebounding in a flash
of light off residences forever reflecting heaven's love-
   affair with earth yet tenderly creating memories of this
scene within us the way it was when we marveled together
   at foot-bridges arches narrow streets shops making masks
the four golden horses on San Marco's balcony the mosaic
   Christ in glory scenes drawing us back a magnet doubly
subject to stellar poles apart together invisible workings
   of irresistible beauty merging mystery into indelible marks
of an earthy transcendence in our souls one indissoluble
   unpartable eternal love within the setting so lovely beside
others before and after us as long as Venice exists on earth

VII VENICE VIA TURNER

Your window's opposite the lagoon looking
over the open sea while what you're working on
   both hides reveals holds back discloses since
such secretive intensity is part and parcel of your
   peculiar gift as an artist honoring beloved places

90

though a public figure such a secretive elusive self
   known best by those nearest and dearest embedded
in places you've loved though now working solo
   against time trying to prevent evaporation from
happening before the paint dries and revisions become
   impossible since the clock will soon strike midnight
while the moon reappears from clouds over the lagoon
   yet such longing you possess for eastern dawn's
dissolving night thus make of first light time to quickly
   leave your studio and draw the day till your heart's
content though concentrated so much you sweat or are
   those tears when drawing your lover of long ago first
found by a friend in your sketch book tentative incomplete
   struggling to capture the magical beauty of person and
place who cares does it matter if you carried an eraser
   in your pocket knowing in advance imperfection was
inevitable after all only the Creator can render true likeness
   to his/her creation and if asked would we spend our lives
knowing ahead we'd always fall short yet you ventured forth
   daily surrendering yourself in communion to transfigure
earthy physical scenes into something profoundly spiritual
   in ways only color and shape can achieve pardon my praise
your being beyond needing such yet my wish to say we are
   changed by seeing things through your eyes and shaped
by your adoring hands as you created Venice in all her glory

VIII KEATS, HAMPSTEAD AND ROME

the sycamore's golden leaves were falling by
   the path that October afternoon when Joe
and I arrived at Keats's Hampstead Heath home
   a copy of his poetry in my purse purchased
at San Francisco's City Lights Bookstore now
   after Joe has passed over a few stray leaves
fall to the floor from the book reminding me of

91

Keats's courage weaving Fanny's love in lines
of loss felt in stanzas sustaining him when they
    were apart we stood side by side that Autumn
under the sycamore overseeing his heath perhaps
    that time he heard the magical nightingale soon
before sailing from home to Italy in hope of healing
    we held hands feeling his spirit close when we
prayed round the bed where Keats died in Rome
    that melancholy October day in his apartment
overlooking the Spanish Steps sound of Bernini's
    fountain below and doves hovering in a wainscot
under the roof of a nearby restaurant where we
    toasted Keats and Fanny's loving memory . . .

IX HARRIMAN STATE PARK, NEW YORK
in memory of my brother Richie Cook

silvery lichen lace wrappers round oaks
    by the path's pockets of melting snow,
paw prints of raccoons and foxes along
    the patio since this is Harriman State
Park's Seven Lakes region bordering
    my brother Richie's home, where he
and his wife Loretta raised six children,
    then welcomed grandkids who love
exploring the woods, a paradise unlike
    our growing up on a run-down street
in Flatbush Brooklyn, but blest we were
    by Prospect Park for sleigh-riding,
row-boating, running wild and free
    through thickets, tunnels, taking
trails down to the zoo, climbing maple
    trees on Lookout Hill, though I never
knew my brother's favorite tree till he
    came to California and we were walking
round Santa Clara's city park, he stopped

92

suddenly: "Look across the lake! See
the most beautiful tree in all the world:
    a weeping willow!" Though we settled
on different coasts, every week we spoke,
    when warm weather he'd chat relaxing
on his deck, catching up on family news,
    books, politics, the church and sometimes
my challenges as a widow, he the kindest
    listener, offering down-to-earth advice if
I asked for feedback and we'd always wind
    up laughing, then in his last years an intense
interest in our ancestors likely linked to his
    deep faith in a loving afterlife reunion, now
looking back at such a thoughtful adventurous
    brother, who understood instinctively as if
a twin, not needing many words, not tooting
    his horn, simply living what he believed:
devotion to family, faith, friends, community,
    co-workers in the company he founded,
helping anyone in need without fanfare, how
    hard saying goodbye that last day, I walked
his street to the forest trail, sparrows in berries,
    robins on lawns, squirrels leaping in maples
as the wintry fog faded, the sun clear of clouds
    lit the far shore across the lake where a weeping
willow waved silvery wands as if angel wings . . .

X INVERNESS, CALIFORNIA

a mother deer is coaxing her young up the hill
    tiny white-tipped tails bobbing as they leap
over a thicket of raspberry brambles while
    the sun and fog feels as if we're present at
the world's first morning seeing lovely lichen
    wands dangle on spongy green moss while

93

an oak grove bends in song we wander by
    picking up our pace following the trail down
to a meadow splashed with fennel and golden
    reeds shimmering round a marsh that seems
rising to welcome incoming tides below the foot-
    bridge we're crossing where winter rains carved
silvery circles on oaken planks near fossil cliffs
    holding earth's history close plus pockets of
puddled pools with rainbowed sea anemones breathing
    in and out while back at the cottage we pick purple
wild irises for the kitchen window then relax sipping
    red wine munching on crackers with hummus before
dinner lights out early no tech gadgets our humming
    encircles each other dreaming and drifting under
a canopy of planets across the heavens seeing the moon
    smiling through the skylight above our bed as though
promising love lasts a lifetime and more so on our way
    to the car next morning forget-me-nots along the path

IV. SPIRITS GALORE

NOTRE DAME

seven doves dive through clouds honey bees
   hover in clover stars spin as a milky-way choir
is singing alleluias gargoyles smile mischievously
   angels leap over the transept former foes dare join
in the kiss of peace reconciliations proliferate path-
   ways of forgiveness multiply enough mea culpas
to go round for all of us imperfect creatures as patient
   Notre Dame welcomes every one over centuries with
a listening heart's refuge believing in each one's good
   faith intentions encouraging a step back from certainty
openly dare share with strangers celebrating liturgies
   led by children dancing down the aisle even if storms
threaten while we recall terrible fires in the forest rafters
   nearly destroying this sanctuary She rose as a phoenix
from ashes resilient recovery slowly surely standing tall
   towers overseeing the Seine's flowing peacefully as birds
fly back to secret buttress nests we snuggle beneath night's
   covers curling up with a partner or solo never alone since
Love's perpetual presence sprinkles benediction waters
   awaking dawn's ascension in rainbowed rose windows

IS POETRY IMPORTANT FOR YOU?
in memory of Galway Kinnell

sometimes dreams and memories dissolve
   by dawn, or out of the blue, a residue

remains, fragments pop up in our psyche,
   extracting an essence, distilling insights,
perhaps a healing potion, the way pollen
   sticks to a bee's feet populating flowers
thus bringing beneficial stuff back to
   the hive's cooperative building project
abuzz with sweetly potent honey, do I dare
   compare poetry to buzzing bees, perhaps
if a line here or there sticks to your mind
   heart or soul not mine now but yours
springboard into your own love of life,
   as happened via the brilliant 17th century
poet John Donne whom I read at Brooklyn
   College, when I was fresh from the convent,
shocked at such explicit sexual love poetry
   under veneers of metaphysical metaphors
transposed in his later years towards devotion
   to Divinity now my around about path of
saying, dear reader, I hope you'll give past
   poets a chance alongside modern ones to
make a difference in whatever way is possible,
   as I recall Galway Kinnell, when Naomi Clark,
fine poet and founder of the San Jose Poetry
   Center, asked me to drive him to a scheduled
workshop, so on the way my naïve question:
   "Galway, is poetry important for you?" Pausing
patiently he said: "Well, Carolyn, poetry has
   saved my life." I rest my case as attorneys say . . .

PAN OF THE FOREST

legendary shimmering golden-clothed creature
   leaping over brambles disappearing in twilight's
forest seen romping by moonlight grape juices
   dripping down beard a leafy laurel wreath round

96

pointed ears playing pipe tunes tapping hooves
    keeping time on damp earth rubbing furry
shoulders on brambles pawing a pebbly path
    dust swirling miniature halos taking a break
summery nap near a spring suddenly wide awake
    jumping over hedges vanishing in the shadows
tiny tawny tufts left on my lips I wonder did we kiss?

RED-TAILED HAWKS

red tails
swim high
swoop round
dive down
left middle right
I'm an awestruck
city kid in the Catskills
watching them scan the fields
shimmering black wings coasting currents
between heaven and earth
tiny white feathers
round black neck
golden eyes
sharp beak
singing
dawn to
dusk
!!

ANGEL FOR A DAY, MONT-SAINT-MICHEL

if I were an angel for a day I'd spin as a compass atop
    Mont-Saint-Michel (though in "real life" I fear heights)
so scanning sea and coast while my damp feathers dry
    in summer sun as I lick salty lips enjoying clouds
rumbling like clowns over cobblestone streets in this

97

town where myths rise and fall for centuries stirring
desire in couples sipping Bordeaux before tumbling
in bed as high tide rises over rocks submerging
sandbars leaving marks in human hearts' memories
flying back to the island's sighting an angel above
the church in a perch is how I got started thinking
about blowing blessings like kisses brandishing
a harmless sword while watching tides gallop as in
long-ago legends when knights and knaves rode
horses between tides now we walk on the sand when
waters are low hear the church bell ring for worship
. . . all are welcomed by monks with the Kiss of Peace

HOPE SPRINGS ETERNAL

after all is said and done the flamed tongue
Dove descends multiplying love's languages
humming hearts renewing ancient legends Pan's
pipe Apollo's harp Aphrodite's affection Eastern
Mages delightful down to earth donkey carrying
a mother birthing in a stable prophet rejected by
powerful rulers first facing fate alone comforted
by a good thief's kind words plus poet Shelley's
reassuring lines: "if winter comes, Spring is not far
behind" soon the swallows return to Capistrano
bees continue pollinating so create healing Manuka
honey mushroom therapies potentially purify
polluted waters enhancing human immunity while
good news California's almost extinct eagles now
sighted in the high-tech Bay Area miracles happen
happily Pan's sacred caves recently rediscovered
in war ravaged Syria burnt offerings incense flowers
ah Ravenna's mosaics and Roman catacomb murals
featuring the Good Shepherd carrying lost lambs home

MEDITATING ON MILTON'S *PARADISE LOST*

years ago, fresh from the convent in a Brooklyn College
    literature class, reading Milton's *Paradise Lost,* I felt
shock, unable at the time to sympathize with Satan and

his fallen angel friends doomed to hellish fires forever,
    yet such extraordinary intelligent beautiful beings
equal to the heavenly hosts, so I was surprised finding

these beings grieving together due to a shared fateful
    flaw of rebelling against strict set rules, costing loss
of everything near and dear, thus once-upon-a-time

noble creatures wallowing in eternal exile far from their
    heavenly home, watched over by a blind poet's inner
eye of compassion, challenging readers to dare examine

our conscience as to whether we so called enlightened
    ones look down on those we're convinced are full of
faults, flaws, evil, so cast outside our community care

by a self-serving superiority projecting our shadow far
    from self and friends, content with conflicts even civil
wars, no pardons permitted, yet who knows for certainty

if a purgatory exists for Satan and his comrades, after all
    who are we to discern Divinity's designs for peace,
forgiveness, reconciliation with the most hopeless . . .

FOUR FANTASTIC FRIENDS
Aileen Cleary, Natalie Budny,
Doreen Norman, Judy Hanley-Mauro

. . . my almost ecstatic foolish unrealistic hope
    I'll see Aileen Natalie Doreen Judy walking
down the street the ways we were when believing

99

angels existed as guardian spirits for as long as
we lived better blest by four wonderful friends

      . . . beautiful brilliant mischievous Aileen
grade school classmate who delighted in disobeying
   rules as No Talking or laughing in class or church
which she gleefully did and I sometimes hesitantly
   went along with her antics as once after Mass
made to pray the Act of Contrition together aloud
   at a long table in the somber convent dining room
an added chance for Aileen to act as a clown
   winking over her hands when the strict Sister
supervising our penance turned her back Aileen
   also showed me how to shimmy down a high
narrow space between two garages and casually
   gave advice about likely "period" coming soon

Natalie best friend in high school who thought
   anything and everything I/she/we did together
as when riding the Flatbush Avenue bus home from
   our school near the Brooklyn Bridge she got off first
by the busy intersection at Church Avenue the back
   bus door stayed open long riders transferring as
Natalie stayed on the sidewalk shouting to passengers
   near me: "Look out for that girl: she's a thief!" some
backed away looked at me suspiciously most smiled
   since Natalie couldn't control her snorting laugh
I know not a nice thing to mention since if I were
   a Black girl who knows what awful reaction might
have happened Natalie begged me to spray water
   on girl messengers from the principal's office who
came to our classroom delivering something for our
   teacher consequently Miss Mulgrew who taught
English nicknamed me "Esmeralda the wild one"

100

Doreen was my visionary mystical friend who
confided her "experiences" of Christ in the way
    teenagers talk about boyfriends sharing stories
of a similar spiritual kind we both believed in plus
    she was down to earth genuinely thoughtful with
a humble wisdom equal to meditation teachers
    that I'd hear decades later she companioned me
after school to a home for children of unwed parents
    such tender care she gave holding little girls close
Doreen entered a teaching community far away from
    the convent I entered my final memory of her is
at my father's funeral when saying goodbye she
    was walking down a familiar Brooklyn street on
her way back to the bus for Long Island then she
    and said: "Cookie, I want you to know I'll be
entering the Carmelites Cloister next month."

Judy was my earliest friend oldest of eleven in
a warm Irish-American family hosting parties for
    baptisms communions confirmations graduations
blest with the family gift for singing as her father
    Mr. Hanley opened the party with "Danny Boy"
followed by Judy Barbara and me doing a song/dance
    routine we created and together went to countless
movies in our Flatbush neighborhood then walking
    home Judy taught the film's songs and lucky me
going to the same camp with her for many summers

    . . . sad to say Aileen died at age 18 when I was in
the novitiate never learned the details and Natalie
    passed over from a heart attack at age 53 so far
impossible to locate Doreen since her Brooklyn
    Carmelite cloister closed thankfully my first dear
friend Judy and I stay in touch via email and phone
    calls between New York and California as I pray
memory's childhood haven may endure for every one

ANGEL OF BETHESDA, CENTRAL PARK, NEW YORK

she refused to defend her reputation simply
    gave-in gave-up that last day in Central Park
taking an unfamiliar path leading to the Angel
    of Bethesda's comforting site offering reminder

of long ago familiar Prospect Park's maples elms
    hickories willows waving while taking turns
with her brothers rowing round the lake that
    summer before she and dear friend Natalie

entered convents far from each other thus their
    last adventure seeking the Shakespeare festival
one summer night in Central Park together lost
    then found by local police driving to nearby

subway back to Brooklyn lots of laughs heading
    home though decades later during a midlife
crisis coming to the angel's legendary fountain
    symbolizing for many New Yorkers a healing

place following failures disappointments illness
    whatever hurts a literary friendship gone south
pulling personal confidence apart at the seams
    so she wished her high school friend were alive

as an angel-like confidante companion yet dearly
    present by this fountain in beloved city of birth
airborne turning over the Atlantic coast curving
    west with the welcoming sun homeward bound

ELUSIVE ENCHANTERS

forest mists crushed pine needles golden fur
    on fences breezes blowing maple leaves

hooded eyes glowing lambs leaping loving
lips blowing farewell kisses reed pipe tunes
paw prints proof in dampened earth once
upon a time dancing with Pan dressed as
someone you loved clouds shrug shoulders
thundering doubts flash across the scientific
horizon loss of life is real mourning doves at
dawn match our feelings rain-drenched bushes
weeping willows night's protective blanket
beneath winter's secretive snow dreams of
Spring below the surface fields reseeding
pregnant dandelion puffs smiling brooks
babbling you are not alone whispering pines

WINTER'S LONGINGS

harsh winds howl frozen branches store
wintry losses weigh down boughs trying to
trust tiny signs of Springs' former hibernating
ways as it was last year when frozen fields melted

streams again were singing with April showers
May flowers abloom wild fields abuzz with bees
nests of fledglings overflowing songs of joy and
even though we mumbled complaints among

ourselves during cold December nights as
sleds coasted close in snow bears snored loudly
beneath boughs till slowly steadily little by
little dawn drew down her thrilling beams of

warmth over us the way Love's powers revive
lost loved ones resurrected in memory or face to
face again as if a miracle after separation such
surprising reunion sharing meals together again

TINY TIPPED EARS

sunlight slips through silvery green willow
   wands alongside rows of roses hawks
coasting dark clouds and I can't help falling
   in love with your adorable irresistible story
popping up at unexpected times and places
   as when I hear rustling raspberry brambles
see tiny delicate tipped ears twitching by a tree
   find tufts of fresh fur stuck on grape vines
feel earth tremble beneath prancing hooved feet
   keeping time with pines whispering hosanna
to the highest grape stains on stones twinkling
   eyes irresistible smile going straight to my heart
gloriously golden pipe music overcoming doubt

FORGET-ME-NOTS

flute music penetrating forest paths piercingly
   beautiful tunes accompanying quicksilver spirits
on their journeys echoing Eros-Psyche's love tufts
   of fur flying on forest floor Merlin's magical art
Hermes/Mercury hidden in alcoves Venus may
   arrive at high tide welcoming back the banished
at borders of belief guardians spirits glimpsed in
   bushes cloven faun footprints lambs' wool
scarves Saint Bernard's brandy Easter lilies owls
   at sunset forget-me-nots Findhorn folks dancing
under stars Nevada desert's annual Burning Man
   celebrations come with me let's leap over bonfires

STRAY SHEEP

once-upon-a-time Pan's pipe celebration
   echoed in Mediterranean cliff caves as dear
down-to-earth faun was honored by shepherds
   praying for lost sheep perhaps live-streaming

sense of humor knowing well human flaws
   yet these our ancestors possessed boundless
belief in Nature's spiritual interrelatedness so
   if hearing the baa baa of prodigal flocks they
ran to swing open the gate for a warm welcome

VENI CREATOR SPIRITUS

Come Holy Spirit make our hearts your dove-cot
   home hovering over past, present, future dawn's
delightful song, night's shimmering cloak of comfort,
   gifting courage after storms, sprinkling compassion

over countless cast into cold indifference, all welcome
   to the banquet table, opposite sides reconciled, good
intentions presumed, disbanding attacks on another's
   motives, cease-fire prevails, preventing what we think

is the worst of others by nipping it in the bud, time for
   self-examination calling for mea culpa, mea maxima
culpa, forgiveness multiplying like seeds in wild fields
   of Spring, circle dances pop up, winter's hibernation's

over, once endangered eagles soar over Pacific coastal
   mountains, turtle doves sighted carrying olive branches
of peace across borders to all regardless of politics, love
   multiplying in little acts starting with me and you . . .

GUARDIAN ANGELS OF THE FOREST

sea spraying a low stone wall bordering rockroses
   green lawns vacation homes a pine grove lining

105

the road leading to a footbridge crossing a stream
   down to where the town square is surrounded by

maples witnessing and whispering secrets they
   overhear when someone is saying *I love you*

under huddling hickories no worries wave lines
   of quaking aspens while willows are weeping

for what is waiting ahead at the bend of the road
   unexpected endings happen hints sprinkled here

and there yet it's easy speaking from experience
   to misread messages looking back over year of

rain/drought winter/summer song/silence hello
   /goodbye success/failure belief/doubt solitude/

community sickness/health love/loss death/birth
   add your spices to the mix as mourning doves at

dawn wake us from slumber after dreaming of Eden
   a final glance back before waking from what was

inexplicably worth the sacrifice since rarely do we
   know the risks becoming clay in the love potter's

hands true choices=consequences ya de da for sure
   yet discernment can be terribly inhibiting lovely

rainbows after storms pines standing as perpetual
   sentinels of good will no matter our failures and

falls swans swimming the shore owls calling at dusk
   nest watched over by guardian angels of the forest

RECYCLING RESURRECTIONS, CHINESE MEDICINE

gently healing with moxa* heat treatments as
   Chinese medicine does the way warm weather
brings life back to dormant plants so it is we
   they you me us others rise as it were from
dust start fresh putting aside harsh judgments
   suspending analysis tolerating imperfection
going easy on mistakes after all a brilliant beauty
   of a star sets in December's solstice sky even
when howling winds frighten eventually seas
   will calm mustard flowers fill fields bees begin
propagating beyond our expectations as butterflies
   burst cocoons mountains may even move without
our noticing love's potent powers no matter time or
   distance the spirit blends dearness in matters of
the heart and soul mini miracles happen without
   our noticing a mother phoenix rises from ashes
feeds the young from her heart mourning doves
   call across the glen nightingales sing stems peek
through humus Easter lilies lovers leaning inside
   a burnt redwood forest rebirth after devastating
fires let's hug before it's too late forget differences
   mycelium webs work silently mending earth's
pollution seasons take turns recycling resurrections . . .

THE GREEN SHADE

An unexpected poet-friend's kindness for
A few hours' dark intelligent eyes sensitive
Enchanting smile casual teasing laughing
Daydreaming forgetful of self learning details
Of another's life blessed time passes too quickly
When having fun recalling adventures within
A public garden beside burnt sienna zinnias
In the green shade across the lawn as nearby

Golden stamen dust shone on black bees' feet
Dark brown coats of deer gleamed in the field
Letting our imaginations roam leap wherever
We wished while enjoying jasmine tea and scones
Spread with raspberry jam as our love for poetry
Poured off the tips of our tongues nonstop though
We knew Autumn was round the corner maple
Leaves in undeterred golden glory about to fall
Sunset colors gathering in apple boughs heavy
Ripened fruit about to be picked and far-off calls
Of the mourning doves when we last walked
Around the lake before taking leave now years
Later rereading lyrical lines beating your heart's
Cadences composed for someone dearly loved
And lost too young before either of you had
A chance at least to call and say goodbye . . .

IF AMONG FALLEN ANGELS

if I were a fallen angel with singed wings
   and tattered feathers grieving alongside
comrades who tumbled head over heels

   into punishing fires, I'd not forget how
fine things were before our rebellion went
   too far, since we ignored how coming into

being was not our doing, brought to life by
   divine design, shouldn't we be grateful at
least we weren't acting like self-righteous

   know-it-alls looking down contemptuously
on us fallibly fragile ones who were once upon
   a time beloved companions in kinship with

our likenesses radiant genes though overturned
   by serious faults, thus perpetual punishment,
forgiveness forbidden the story says and yet why

   not a truce, reprieve, admit possibility you too
could have fallen from grace, though humans
   given a second change in purgatorial fires for

purging past mistakes, why not prodigal angels
   welcome home too, generously extent pardons
to all who wish so with wings humbly folded

   returning prodigals to paradise, merciful welcome
back for each and all, none excluded, even so-called
   fallen angels, like exiled humans or lost sheep

FAUN AT THE PANTHEON

Light shining on forestry faun fur, as you peek
   through shadowy boughs of a weeping willow.

Cloven feet tapping a tune. Pointed ears twitching.
   Fleecy coat glistening. White spot on forehead

twinkling where your spirit shall pass over someday
   into a forestry faun heaven. Now mischievously

smiling creature, I offer pitted cherries as a treat.
   Thanks for letting me stroke behind your ears.

Though born in the wild long-ago legends say in
   faraway places, you jump suddenly into scenes

when most in need, disguised domesticated as
   a household pet. Or as a sure-footed creature

109

in the forests of our childhood and along paths
   hiked in middle age, plus sightings in our elder

years in the backyard or park, dearly mischievous
   one met with my deceased husband along trails

disappearing in shadows or when I'm on retreat
   at a California monastery, I've seen you dart

about the brambles of Big Sur appearing around
   the call to Compline, you leap over ferns, rejoin

cloven clans dancing with laurel leaf crowns, enjoy
   chestnuts, apple cider, berries, honeyed wine

dripping from your lips, green-black eyes flashing
   fun, ears twitching as you prance on stones over

streams, trot through storms, offering lost souls
   guidance home with your enchanting flute music

ODE TO CARAVAGGIO

Remembering Caravaggio's struggles, sufferings,
his talent, passions, his shock at being betrayed,

losing his temper, so seeking violent revenge
resulting in police pursing him from Rome to

wherever he found refuge in towns, villages
throughout southern Italy, perpetually moving,

yet managing to paint canvasses, till eventually
seeking home, he died alone on a deserted beach

110

as the ship sailed in the distance, though some
canvasses rolled together traveled to a benefactor

cardinal, as a painting of beheaded anguished
John the Baptist, resembling his self-portrait,

how many more canvasses he could have
created if not dying so young, such a unique

incomparable earthy sensual spiritual mixture
as seen in Bacchus's gleeful smile flaunting

sexuality or such tender pathos portraying
Christ's handsome forehead pierced painfully

by a crown of bloody thorns, who can forget
seeing his Saint Paul's muscular body stretched

upside down on a Roman cross, or the strong
Madonna standing barefoot on kitchen steps

with the beautiful baby boy balanced on her hip,
or the painting of Saul struck from his horse,

lying flat on his back full of fear before a magnificent
angel hovering over him along the road to Damascus,

so in spirit I bow in thanksgiving to Caravaggio
alongside those he painted kneeling at the nativity . . .

ONCE-UPON-A-TIME SHEPHERDS

Are you walking the damp earth finding fox's paw prints
    lambs' fur on fences lavender bushes buzzing with bees
sunflowers smiling in your face rustling leaves overhead

soon seeing a shepherd in high-laced sandals on a hill who
looks like a brother to the ancient shepherd-god worshipped
in a Syrian cave overlooking the sea similar to Ravenna's
mosaic created centuries ago of the Good Shepherd carrying
a lamb round his shoulders through a green field dotted by
poppies while lots of lambs frolic close by celebrating rescue
from slaughter as to the left a lion lies down with a lamb

TINTORETTO'S CHRIST

Remember when we were walking the Venetian
shore orange flags fluttering in the wind beside

black bobbing gondolas as cumulus clouds
drifted over the blue sea and sky then we rode

a vaporetto across the Grand Canal soon strolled
twisting streets till inside Scuola San Rocco before

Tintoretto's portrayals of Christ awed in silence
as if in a living church watching the crucified man

turning towards the nearby prisoner whispering
comforting words since friends had fled, reaching

across time promising hope to all condemned by
the world: "Today you'll be with me in Paradise"

DIVINE DISGUISES

divine disguises sometimes take on daring
transformations in us ordinary folks who may
discover/uncover a spiritual trickster good
humor alongside twists/turns doubts/faith
lost/found letting bygones be shaking off

grudges forgiving even if not forgiven shrugging
   shoulders at harsh judgements leave off self-
defensiveness free up cocooned butterflies so
   let's fly low on flowers give a chance to spin
straw into golden garments said the poor girl to
   the trickster Rumpelstiltskin and thankfully she
overheard his hubris dance in moonlight yes let's
   dare follow her example walk through storms
seek silver linings skip down Plato's middle path
   presume a person's good intentions put to rest
crushing guilt whistle a tune join the fox trotting
   sip a buttercup on a cliff overlooking the Pacific

OH LET ME LEARN LILIES OF THE FIELD

oh let me learn to lie down with lilies of the field
listening to little winged ones whistling in grasses

practicing a oneness with whatever floats lands
lifts off lingers long in love's gaze angels daily

disguised in countless costumes at crossroads
when we're lost and most in need no ledger or

keeping score no separation kinship kept close
with every creature human earthly divine simple

complexity spreads across the globe putting aside
judging in a lovely letting go bowing as night falls

we're heading home will curl up as foxes in dens
birds nesting bees in hives now I lay me down to

sleep daydreaming with the seasons taking turns
paradise lost re-found fanning hope nurturing

113

underground meditation seeds just being who we
are born to be flawed and all waking after winter's

frost such surprises Spring brings filling fields and
highways with lilies trumpeting Easter Alleluias

WINGED ONES

a monarch butterfly's morning surprise stopping by
   briefly before picking up the migration south to

Mexico time to sip rosemary do a solo break dance
   reminding me of pleasures put aside due to routine

pressures placing a lid on novelty conforming to
   group think and behavior not wanting a label of

show-off for thinking/acting outside the box so stay
   close to majority opinion subtle censoring as it may

unconsciously be don't dare say something contrary
   though I did once or twice upon a time surprise others

by my actions not to compare me to this winged one in
   the garden dancing wildly among flowers yet brings

back a day I wore a red sweater gray-blue blouse jeans
   and sneakers seen in long-ago photo when I blithely

followed the one I loved into a forest without a care in
   the world no need for future plans since enchanted

by a daring take on love's risks without a second thought
   though to be honest my adventurous spirit left a lot to be

114

desired after I left Brooklyn for a religious community
   thus setting in motion my more conventional persona

plus chalk it up to getting older as we all "must" do
   though I admit a serious transgression did happen

causing a public shaming which left an inhibiting mark
   if not concerning caution even when composing poems

which Robert Bly at a workshop warned poets "never
   allow a censor to sit on your shoulder" though likely

I have so needing today's simple surprising butterfly
   sipping lavender in the garden as a sweet discreet

no pressure teacherly reminder of spontaneity's child
   within who loves leaping in fields of wildflowers

TRANSFIGURATION

. . . typically thoughtful, You invited us to
   come along on a hike, though cautioned

it wouldn't be easy, turned out exhausting,
   and capped by a surprise at the summit

revealing a sweeping view of the valley with
   the lake of Galilee shimmering amid palms

and olive groves, flocks of sheep in fields, birds
   circling in warm air currents below, I heard

a swishing upsweep of wind and turned to see
   You rising off the mountain and I confess feeling

afraid, wondering if this was an illusion due to
the afternoon heat, no one said a word, then

suddenly a swarm of bees round Your shoulders,
a lamb leapt out of a bush and a dove descended

from clouds, thunder rumbled in rocks under us,
flashes of lightning close by as Your entire self

transfigured into a luminous Being we knew and
didn't know, so we all fell down, hiding our faces

from the blazing light, waiting in fear till You
calmly came back to earth and called us close,

as if nothing unusual had happened, though I felt
a static electricity clinging to Your clothes as we

all pretended nothing special had happened while
heading downhill, some of us whispered about

what we witnessed of Your rising several feet above
close to clouds, I said nothing, stunned in silence,

soon we settled down near the lake where John
and James cooked fish and shared flasks of wine

and to this day I can't say if this event happened
before or after You died, nor do I know what if

any teaching was intended, unless a tangible way
to comfort us since You would be going beyond

the great divide, but before that final leave taking
this kindly parting the veil dividing the so-called

tangible tangled world of existence from the ethereal
other side beyond reach, though lacking proof, yet

I recall how it was when You rose transfigured in
the sky way before we began drinking the wine . . .

TURNING POINT

. . . so it is, was, will be engraved in my psyche,
our respectful honesty coming together promising
a friendship faithful to those we love, agreeing in
advance on clear boundaries, accepting limitations
. . . I was recovering, my life in tatters, you offered
healing help sensing my reality without needing many
words. Your initial kindness at lunch with a mutual
friend, both of us far from home. I listened as you two
talked, then you turned: "And what is your work
Carolyn?" No one ever inquired so sincerely, as if
a mini miracle opening a blessed friendship, even
though a sacrifice of some precious research time in
America. Our affinity taught me a lasting lesson,
how compassion can spring into action after loss,
if care's given without prejudice to past offenses,
spreading hope as a healing cloak over brokenness
allowing time to get on one's feet again, restore
self-confidence in God's plan while we attend as
well to loved ones who matter more than ever . . .

A MEETING MADE TO OUTLAST LOSS

It was late October in middle America when
they strolled through the city park one
Sunday afternoon while light rain was falling

on their way to the city museum, having
just left his rented basement apartment whose
street-level windows looked up at rows of

117

golden maple leaves while the ledge back in
the bedroom with all the notes she wrote
him this past year on display making her blush

since such thoughtfulness was an unexpected
sight she needed without knowing the need
till later in the museum standing by El Greco's

Christ struggling to discern his future path in
the Garden of Gethsemane, she felt similarly
confused, though not threatened by death,

instead stuck in a Limbo of doubt, seeking
a spiritual clarity in the midst of cloudy choices,
while trying to live "one day at a time," blest

by his affirmations healing her broken heart,
needing a protective cloak for future courage
as she readied to head home, a subject of public

scandal, unable to clear her name, yet comforted
by their agreement in advance, a temporary healing
closeness, honoring prior commitments, such an

honest trust rare and risky, if either one became too
attached, but both deliberately disciplined believing
it was not accidental how they met, so a final farewell

accepted gracefully before leaving for the airport,
she waved goodbye through the taxi window while
he stood smiling under golden maples dripping rain

SHIMMERING SIGNS

Memories swirl as I pick up flecks of golden
sand where we used to walk when high tide

blew inland across the ocean. Clouds darkened
  an inlet. Doubt fled from faith. The world
seemed shimmering with divine signs. I tried
  staying steady, which I did and didn't do,
depending on graces others gave or withheld.
  Stars were shooting across a summer sky.
Soon a thunderstorm. I slipped on a murky
  side path. Guardrails broke at the shore.
Rockroses tore. I phoned a poet friend, who
  insisted with a smile "this as everything else
is grist for the mill in our profession." So empty
  pages wait daily. Recipe for memory's potluck
stew. "Look for the silver lining" Legends of loss
  linger, trying to spin dross into golden threads
weaving mistakes into helpful winter garments,
  easier said than done, yet faith presses forward
grateful for past poets distilling extracts for each
  reader as in herbal healing, doses drawn from
negative/positive stuff through threads of lines/lives

TO BELIEVE OR NOT TO BELIEVE
In an interview in his last years C.G. Jung was asked:
  "When you were a child, did you believe in God?"
  "Why, yes, I believed as a child." "Do you still believe
  now?" "Well, I do not need to believe, I know."

Oh, Love Divine, appearing benevolently kind
  when I was growing up in Flatbush Brooklyn
              enjoying feast days
              of saints galore in
our parish church lit up elaborately in celebration
  with candles and flowers filling the sanctuary
              with earthly mysterious
              personal pleasures
as sacred rituals were sprinkled throughout the year
  Christmas Easter Pentecost incense bells hymns
              Ordinary or Solemn
              High Mass climaxing

119

when sacred words possess power to change bread
   and wine into Christ's body and blood a miracle
                  for all to taste
                  within as I did
for the first time at age seven awestruck and happy
   indelibly marked by Divine intervention in ordinary
                  me you we us
                  all together now
daily possessed by God's personal presence in our
   uniquely unfathomable tabernacles within . . .

FOREST FORGIVING

warm air maple trees turning a golden red
   while we were swimming before dinner since
summer lingered into early evening my mistakes
   were several projecting on to Nature promises
of good things to come as the pine trees glistened
   calmly dawn to dusk their dark green branches
waving in mostly clear blue skies so I typically
   ignored dark clouds gathering over the horizon
not reading too much into greetings by townsfolk
   when shopping for groceries though grateful
for any positive signs to discern seeing churches
   on "the green" offering encouragement that
things would turn out well for all concerned
   in the end how wrong I was about what would
happen thus an abrupt break unintended by me
   on both coasts no exceptions to the rules thus
set in place beyond my doing plus I fumbled
   with lame excuses though underneath it all I
(foolishly?) held on to Joseph Campbell's words
   as a calling: "Follow your bliss" so regardless
of what did or did not happen I remain grateful
   to that glorious forest of birches pines elms
spruces maples laurels hickories witnessing

the best I gave though flawed and imperfect
self-defense well-intentioned strong sentinels
  of unconditional loving forgiveness hallelujah

DEAR DOVES

dear doves ascending descending letting us
  look over your shoulders ride outspread
wide wings with homing pigeons plus playful
  mischievous messengers surfing earth's seas
discerning directions to offer us pathways when
we've lost our way through dense forests to
  help bring us back to the safe harbor sighted
so rediscover home's warm delightful nest again

INTERCESSIONS, NEW YORK CITY

. . . from a Jesuit friend's dining room, he points
  to an apartment across the street where a famed
pianist is practicing for an up-and-coming Carnegie

  Hall recital does she wonder if this community
prays for a successful performance her background
  is Catholic perhaps I'm reading into the fact that

she doesn't draw the drapes near her piano maybe
  wishing to be seen working hard at her vocation
which brings me to the point of this poem whether

even highly talented people who work diligently at
  their profession feel the need for people to pray
that their performances be blest who knows if she

is aware that these nearby Jesuits may be praying on
  her behalf while she trusts in the God who gave
this gift at the start calling for hard work her entire life

knowing perfection's elusive so in need of prayer as all
in the arts are my poet friend and I included inspired
by hearing Alicia de la Rocha practicing hours and hours

so he listens and prays which is his way in the world
to notice anyone in need of assistance thus I dared to
send him an SOS email for help to finish this book

which he generously agreed to proof read and offer
gentle helpful editorial advice I bow in thanks
to gifted generous prayerful poet: James Torrens S.J.

CONSIDER CHRIST'S TOMB

. . . the door, entrance, opening between
stones, avenues into the inner chambers,
resting places for countless souls . . .
consider Christ's tomb carved in stone,
Ramses buried in an earthen cave over
3,000 years ago, grandma's Orkney
ancestors' stone circles, Mission Santa Clara,
Brooklyn's Holy Cross cemetery . . .
the need, desire, wish for continued
contact with loved ones who've passed over,
not to break the link, rather attend rituals,
remember, create and explore chambers
of memory as Matteo Ricci described in detail
setting up shrines with familiar pictures
of the deceased, bring candles, aromatic
plants . . . remembering when you asked
Joe shortly before he passed over: "Would
you like me to read some Scripture passages?"
he smiled and silently pointed to his heart,
the brilliant scholarship, tender devotions,

meditations, writings, wounds, healings . . .
were Jesus's friends ready for his passing . . .
   seems unlikely given his relative youth,
   similarly, my father dying too young yet
memory can construct places where loved
   ones are prayed to . . . perhaps poetry's
   possible quest seeking words, lines, stanzas
places to pause featuring hope, faith, love . . .

ALLELUIA FOR C.G. JUNG

   dare I admit believing in divinely
mischievous beings who get a kick
   out of turning things upside down
inside out hiding directions when we
   were sure of knowing the path even
encouraging us to make mistakes take
   a dose of bitter medicine eat portions
of humble pie following a public shaming
   perhaps teaching compassion in a round-
about way archetypal timeless stories
   helpful in sorting through experiences
especially if painfully felt as arrows of
   judgment piercing your persona yes
deeds done wrongly especially if you
   go against the grain of good behavior
even if excuses are made perhaps silence
   is the better defense along with confiding
in a compassionate counselor or friend so
   best by finding Jung's "The Undisclosed
Self" in my bookcase noticing how I marked
   the text yet retained no memory of reading it
though Marie Louise von Franz's comment
   comes to mine when someone asked her
what she thought was important to remember

about a lecture she had delivered . . . well
paraphrasing that wise Jungian therapist:
  "Trust you will remember what you need
at the time. Another person will find something
  else relating to their concerns. What sticks for
you is what was necessary." So Jung's text seems
  fresh and relevant each time I open the pages . . .

HELOISE TO ABELARD

since you've been gone for so long the leaves of
  the sweet gum trees began turning scarlet and
golden weeks ago so now they stand almost bare
  in the rainy sky as the chapel doors swing open
beside the serenely lit sanctuary lamp where I pray
  remembering when we last hugged as bells were
ringing for Vespers though I mistook signs of Nature's
  gentleness at the time as a promise our separation
was temporary foolishly believing we'd be again as
  we were thus a late painful lesson in love's infinity
possible only with Divinity though consolation prizes
  come when silvery clouds skipped with the sun over
a pine forest messenger birds return to senders notes
  are answered scintillas of shivering light across green
waters shivers of joy spread when least expected as that
  day you appeared out of the blue beside the convent's
rose garden and were invited to offer Mass before what
  would become without our knowing a final farewell

POMPEII VILLA MYSTERIES
Pompeii Initiation Rites of Women by Kate Bradshaw

she found herself thrust suddenly into the temple
corridor no escape her heart was beating hard
how had this happened where was her guide

she heard a faint drumbeat sounds of footsteps
on flagstones found an open chamber where
murals on walls of animals appeared brewing

an elixir that made horns grow on humans
fur on their bodies and cloven feet while off
to the side a satyr was playing his flute and

a dryad was nursing deer permeating the scene
with a sense of secrecy and filling each space
with a fearful expectation for what might come

next panel featuring someone resembling herself
then the figure of a man looking both to be friend
and stranger and friend what was she to do or say

no clue from others vaguely in the background
waiting with the pain of uncertainty soon a bell
echoing round a corner becoming a labyrinth as

she caught sight of someone she knew briefly ages
ago why now she wondered while surrendering to
a purifying procedure stinging nettles bitter herbs

she looked back at the bearded face in the mirror
near and far coming to the table for communion
weaving ecstasy with loss happily the One she

wanted more than any other dissolved in bread
on her tongue since the basket was handed over
before the resurrection mural with lilies doves

so she laughed and cried confiding faults and
hopes for forgiveness sipping wine held in
the cup while a chorus was chanting Alleluia

AN AMATEUR'S ASTROLOGY ANALYSIS
for the Analytical Psychology Club of San Francisco

. . . maybe the unicorn's related to the goat in
astrology's "Capricorn" possessing practical
   traits, this my birth sign, though I've tended
towards more mythic "unicorn" things, perhaps
   a gene inherited from Orkney Island ancestors
plus my Catholic roots in rituals mixing with
   magical archetypal icons pressing ignorantly
towards welcoming a winged Hermes in a day-
   dream at a crossroads while walking the woods
one summer afternoon, I lost my bearings, cast
   caution to the wind, without a clue or compass
as to "what's next" till eventually a Capricorn
   creature leapt to the rescue nudging me to be
practical: put 2 +2 together, face my mistakes,
   shrug shoulders, swallow pride, head home, ears
attuned to gossip behind my back, tail between legs,
   a public fall from grace, I ate humble pie, faced fateful
consequences, yet wonder if I hear flute music during
   dreams will I simply smile or act a foolish unicorn again . . .

CATSKILL FOREST SPIRITS

silvery-green willow wands shimmering
   pines clouds caressing mountain tops
reeds rising in fog furry figures dash
   through underbrush acres of pristine
Catskill forests city girls away at camp
   Nature hikes folk dancing arts 'n crafts
archery boating/swimming in Silver Lake
   singing at night under the stars golden
feathers flying to nests bees humming in
   raspberry bushes sunset over the valley
we're holding hands bowing to four directions

HERMES AT THE CROSSROADS

coming even if not called
                          mischievous companionable
trickster overturning best
                          laid plans seemingly just
for fun
         yet underneath it all
                          a reliable gentle hearted
guide standing as a stone
                          suggesting directions at
Life's crossroads when
                          we've lost our way home trail
obscured at least two
                          possibilities at once round about
up down spiraling
              back
                     to the beginning
                                 hail known
and unknown contemporary ancient

                              kindly presence
appearing when most needed
                              dressed with feathery cap
wing tipped shoes
                    friend stranger neighbor relative
scattering pebbles
                along
                    the path leading us home

A FRIEND'S FEELINGS FOR PAN

a friend believes Pan was an ancestor of Christ,
   but can't prove her theory, both were worshipped
in lands nearby Palestine and Syria, their followers
   crossing paths in deserts, villages, cities, shrines
where worshippers wove kinship tales till separated
   by hardliners in power structures over centuries, so
Pan fell from favor, as Christ grew in stature following
   Constantine's Roman empire banishing worship of
ancient gods under penalty of death, thus a world rose
   where a divine rustic shepherd wore a cloak, high-
laced sandals once favored by Pan's shepherds guiding
   flocks as portrayed in Ravenna's Sant' Apollinare in
Classe's mosaic of the Good Shepherd standing within
   a green field surrounded by lilies, bees, birds, pines
while He carries a little lamb round his shoulders

ANCIENT ANCESTORS

Legends say Christ's birth banished the long-ago
spirits beloved for centuries, Pan, Hermes, Apollo,
Persephone, Eros, Venus, Athena since certain
Christian rulers fearing rivalry for their newly
anointed God clothed as a child arriving in
the East under a star announced by angels,
who may have happily shared his kindom
with sprites, fairies worshipped in caves,
fields, forests, valleys, mountains, till
cast out by rigid rulers allowing only
a single adored One so ancestors
cast aside followers persecuted
sites abandoned almost entirely
trace memory persists in our
psyche's remnants now
evermore all inclusive
diverse ancestors
Pantocrator
Christ

WHERE YOU SOMETIMES GO

Do You sometimes take flight off our altars
If we keep You solely as an object of worship
Ignoring Your perpetual presence in our lives
So suddenly You fly incognito into our world
Resting from adulation wishing to take up
Residence with unassuming folks among
The homeless farm laborers caregivers
Gardeners assembly-line workers elders
The unemployed widowed orphaned

129

Incarcerated parolees children sick folks
And countless more including yes the lost
Sheep who are despised and scapegoated
While You forgive console lovingly carry
Over Your shoulders with a warm welcoming
Forgiveness while some say they see You
Leaping to the stars leaning over earth for
A comeback of unconditional Love . . .

Recycling Resurrections, Chinese Medicine p. 107 *
   "The complete term is moxibustion, which is the
therapeutic method of burning what is called moxa wool,
the dried, compressed leaves of a species of wormwood
called Artemisia vulgaris latiflora. Small balls or cones of
compressed moxa are burned on or over acupuncture points
or weak injured areas of the body to warm the tissue and
increase local circulation."
Dr. Efrem Korngold, OMD, Chinese Medicine Works,
                              San Francisco, California

130

V. ALCHEMY

THE MYSTIC LAMB
homage to Jan van Eyck's Ghent Altarpiece

. . . in Jan van Eyck's Ghent Altarpiece I worship
   the Mystic Lamb whose divinely human animal
gaze goes straight to my heart and soul amazed
   as I am at this dear creature appearing publicly
just before thousands of people across the globe
   facing a soon to be devastating pandemic perhaps
preparing us in advance with your compassionate
   courage since after centuries You dear Lamb hid
beneath layers of varnish till reappearing now as
   the original vision of the painter thanks to recent
restorers coming to us on the cusp of this world-
   wide crisis confronting millions in a prophetic
coincidence offering a divine creature's presence
   drawing us close to loved ones alongside long ago
worshipers ever hopeful in prayerful appeals for
   healing help so I will continue daily bowing in
adoration at this altar's sacred icon Lamb of God
   who thankfully is set on my computer Desktop
screen conveying a compassionate gaze . . .

BACK TO THE BEGINNING, LAKE RONKONKOMA, LONG ISLAND

even as it was happening at age five
   did I sense unconsciously this might

become a significantly life altering event
   taking time to discern a divine design

that day I dared disobey my father saying
   "Don't come further!" but I took a step

following my older brother before I sank
   into murky deep waters unable to touch

down so swirled round as golden bands
   crisscrossed in warm darkness while I felt

a humming pressure in my ears till suddenly
   my father's strong arms lifted me up to his

shoulders and I saw the high hills on both
   sides surrounding us with tall green trees

so the child I was saved in the nick of time
   carried back to the family blanket along

shore with a large beach towel around me
   beside my mother and grandmother while

both brothers close by looking concerned
   no preaching about what I did in disobeying

just relief for rescue though next time at Riis Park
   Beach not far from our Flatbush apartment

Dad taught me and my brothers survival skills
   in the Atlantic since my having faced death in

that Long Island lake a life-long lesson shedding
   light on listening to words of love's warnings

without overly fearful as a teenager I went on to
  become a Red Cross lifeguard at summer camp

HANSEL AND GRETEL

A low stone wall with sun fading early since winter
Arrived sooner than expected and we became lost
When taking a wrong trail back to town so decided
To spend the night in a wilderness wondering if we
Were resilient enough to enjoy this as an adventure
As when we were young soon dreaming of lost lambs
Leaping for joy on hearing the familiar shepherd
Calling over the hillside which led to another dream
Story of the long-lost prodigal recognized by parents
Far off in the field and they unhesitatingly run with
Open arms of welcome home no guilt trip or chewing
Out reprimand simply glad to see you again come
To the feast table in your honor since once you were
Lost now found such dreams it turned out afterwards
Were dreamt by us both as a synchronicity perhaps
How it was for Hansel and Gretel in the fairy tale
Seeing and hearing fourteen angels hovering over
Them with loving reassurance that all will be well
Likewise we woke refreshed and saw the path parting
To the side of an ancient oak pointing the way home

ATLANTIC WAVES

in the beginning sounds of a rumbling surf
before seeing white crests rising far beyond
the boardwalk railing hot glistening sands

in our growing-up years when the waves rose
and fell between jetties of the public beach
daring us to dive under coming up on the other

side of adventure into temporarily calm sea
before swells rose again on a glimmering horizon
not preventing a daring do it again attitude since

young fearless and foolish as we were yet old
enough for our father's okay since his having
taught us survival skills so we kids went where

we wished into a crashing surf and sometimes
foolishly risking my life arms straight as an arrow
head in a line under a huge roaring wave till

luckily coming up in the calm other side before
riding a roller to shore where grandma was waving
she my source of Scottish Orkney legendary sea

creatures as distant relatives while grandpa sat
in a suit watching under the beach umbrella then
Dad drove us back over the Jamaica Bay Bridge

but before home he'd stop at the Jewish Deli on
Nostrand Avenue to fish out kosher pickles in
a wooden barrel to accompany a Rheingold beer

so years later ushering at San Francisco opera I felt
unconsciously drawn to Wagner's Rhine maidens
singing of a magical golden ring they guarded under

a river's fall perhaps a nostalgic archetypal motif
applicable to all audiences as if we're hypnotized
by early watery adventures primarily being born . . .

MAGICAL ORDINARY FLATBUSH STUFF

Fabulous Loew's Kings on Flatbush Avenue
featuring films that Judy and I adored, *Cinderella,*

134

Snow White, Oklahoma,
South Pacific, The Wizard of Oz
we sang and danced our way home, day-dreams
chock-full of possibilities, easy enough believing
　　　　ordinary bread
　　　　transformed into
Christ's body and blood through the Sacred Words of
Consecration why not a miracle witnessed weekly how
　　　　language more
　　　　than recalls, rather
creates divinity's Real Presence before our attendance,
so we take, taste, nourish self in sharing communion
　　　　with friends and strangers
　　　　peaceful phrases
perhaps subconscious clues of language's powerful
potential to influence hearts and souls to forgive,
　　　　admit mistakes,
　　　　revive fresh starts
like Spring-cleaning letting go preconceived labels
of good and bad, instead come closer to sacred
　　　　simple intentions
　　　　conveyed in childhood
when back-stroking in the pool guided by ceiling lights,
jumping off the board, breaststroke, or seeing jellyfish
　　　　floating up and down
　　　　in Monterey Bay aquarium,
smiling similarities multiply: you, me, we, they,
all together turning cartwheels easy-as-pie for kids,
　　　　summer nights in Brooklyn,
　　　　fireflies in Prospect Park,
Coney Island July 4th fireworks, magnificent west
coast redwoods, email musical birthday cards sent
　　　　by Judy back east,
　　　　renewing friendship
no matter our political positions, such a blessing at
the start hand-in-hand singing and dancing home

on Flatbush streets
  also beside each other
at Mass believing Divinity's in a holy wafer melting
on our tongues Eastside Westside all around the town

CATSKILL IMPRESSIONS

Bees were humming in chamomile clusters
under a clear blue summer sky when I was
  a girl daydreaming in a Catskill mountain
camp during daily rest hour following lunch
  charmed by windy rain silences in nearby
birches poplars pines elms outside the open
  cabin's window daydreams fire-side songs
taking on a life of their own over a meadow
  dotted by black-striped golden bees hovering
happily in wildflowers bluebirds chirping by
  raspberry brambles owls calling across the night
sunrising round Mount Zorn Mother Nature's
  powerful presence in a child's consciousness

SIXTEEN IN THE PHOTO

recently a friend looked at my photo and asked:
  "Why would you choose to enter a convent?!"
impossible to explain this was not a rational
  choice like choosing a career or college who
can say the constellation of things coming together
  in such decisions as I recall the year before entering
the convent I enrolled in a chemistry class at a local
  public high school and met Jackie McC who began
driving me home unforgettable the night he started
  crying and confided that his girlfriend drowned
last summer in a public pool at semester's end he
  asked if we could start dating and I said: "Sorry,
I plan to enter a convent" we parted friends surprise
  at Christmas a lovely bouquet delivered by a florist

with Jackie's card: "Here's for happiness in the future!"
He declined the invitation to my Senior Prom well aware
my heart was set on Christ a suitor no boy could possibly
compete with and win in the end wisely he didn't try . . .

COMPASS OF COMPASSION
in memory of my brother Richie Cook

Recalling when a really rough patch was
happening since a loved one was seriously
   ill and a final end loomed round the corner

which would hit hard since I'd grieve this
   great loss with few who'd know how it felt
yet blessed surprise my brother's reassuring

support throughout my years as a widow and
   then I witnessed great courage in his final
farewell without needing words since he gave

a lifetime of faith hope and loving devotion
   to family friends colleagues community
and prayer an unsung hero with outstanding

down-to-earth wisdom sprinkled with witty
   practical advice and a fantastic sense of
low-key humor so when on rough seas

which happens to most folks at times how
   blest I was as others too by my brother giving
a compass for discerning the way to navigate

towards a home harbor's welcome while I hope
   and pray he sails happily with our ancestors
across the heavens while watching over us . . .

137

THANKSGIVINGS
for Kathleen Hanson

Golden sand blowing in our faces as waves
and wind grew stronger. In hindsight we said

an omen of the looming pandemic. So, such
arrived separating us for months in solitude

except for social distancing visits from family
in my backyard, emails, phone calls and a few

Zooms. Trying as every one else to carry on
remotely. Each day poetry pages sit silently,

smiling, sleeping or waiting for revisions with
a welcoming Hi Let's resume! Some friends are

baking daily. Metaphorically follow their example:
press memories of courage with a pestle, sprinkle

dashes of hope, leaven the dough with patience,
season with trust, bake in a warm oven of affection.

While on the side store seasonings to decrease
stress with healing herbs: straight, diluted, mixed:

elderberry, turmeric, garlic, mint, evening primrose,
chrysanthemums, chamomile lavender's sweet calming

nightcap. Relearning to trust sunrise, sunset, moon,
stars, winter hibernating essential for Spring revival,

so practice seeing summer picnics as before only better
for what we've endured, hopeful for a Thanksgiving reunion

potluck of baked goods galore, gathered with family
and friends round the table, laughing with the children . . .

NATURE'S SILVER LININGS

sparrows nibbling seeds on the forest floor
after fierce storms acorns so abundant pine nuts
a steaming humus greeting golden violet blue

irises rainbowed spider webs and tiger lilies too
sleepy hidden hibernating harvests let's not
forget offshoots of miniature redwoods someday

surprising giants of the forests faithful sentinels
of courage sweet savory sustaining chard onions
peas tomatoes in our gardens while we watch

midwinter sun inch by inch each day's touching
us closer and closer through window sills along
a rosemary bush's tip-top spray of tiniest fair blue

buds of joy shining warmly so earth's perennial
epiphany seen hard at work with bees once again
propagating plants while we humans eagerly

await an okay health signal to be up close once
more with loved ones we've dearly missed so
shall we witness Nature's summer harvest again

COOKING LESSONS

The Indian woman chef is tossing cardamom
into sizzling olive oil, so tiny tight seed shells
burst open brightly in the pan creating a swift

chemical reaction mixing with onions rice
beans beside long gray-green curry leaves, as
   Julia Child standing aside, asks: "What flavor

will they contribute to the dish?" "Why none!
   Curry leaves possess no flavor whatsoever,
only their seeds do. We toss them in not for

   flavor or coloring, but for their aroma. Come
close and smell. There is nothing like them in
   all the world." "Oh marvelous! like unique

popping of cardamom seeds." "Yes, it is so."
   Watching these two talented women working
together, I wonder if mixing people's unique

   views, beliefs, traditions can create a political-
like cuisine combining unusual combinations,
   across the spectrum complementing opposites,

overcoming prejudice, hatred, prompting fresh
   ways of thinking/acting/responding, so
shocking the liberal/progressive, conservative

   mass media with fresh surprising mix of
cooperative cross-pollination benefiting all,
   hopefully halting hostility, so East/West

like cooking combinations creating fresh
   ways to mix opposites benefiting both
and all with tidbits/insights healing families,

   communities, countries across mother-earth
watching in the wings winking/praying we
   foolish folks will try new ways of relating,

as Julia Child stepping aside, listens, learns,
    dialogues with the woman chef from India
mixing ingredients in new ways with the West.

LETTER TO A JAPANESE POET

    . . . years passed since you wrote about
    the woman you loved. No way to know if
she was actually aware of your affection. Once
    upon a time you walked together in a cherry
orchard delighting in pink blossoms rising and
    falling. Suddenly she left for a distant town
across the mountains. Rumor said for an arranged
    marriage. You spent months waiting fruitlessly
for her return. Eventually turning towards monastic
    life devoted to meditation and composing poetry.
A way to honor her presence. So, decades later you
    were laid to rest beneath a cherry tree. Someone
discovered your notebooks, copied the poems on
    rice paper then bound by parchment and painted
the cover with cherry blossoms. A century later
    I found your book, translated into English, on
a shelf in San Francisco's City Lights Bookstore.
    Now I'm learning of your devotion to a lost love
whose memory companioned you till the very end.

POETRY

. . . my poems sometimes seem to go up
    in smoke, hide behind my back like a little
child if I read to someone who says: "I never
    read poetry" which should have been a clue
for me to put my book away, which I didn't do
    that day, due to my stubborn streak mixed
with an idealistic goal of converting someone
    to poetry via my work (is this hubris?) how
foolish I can be, having failed on prior occasions

141

when she changed the subject soon after I read
by beginning to ask about my family, which was
    lovely yet limited since poetry is like kinship
too, so I tend to retreat at times to where many
    poets live on each other's pages, blest I've been
by those past, present, future writers most who've
    hoped labors left behind might someday speak
meaningfully to others down the road, perhaps
    converting a few to our life's work of poetry

AQUINAS'S SUMMA STEW

Why do we usually think things are either right/
Wrong yes/no why not choose a variety of conflicting
Possibilities allowing multiple answers around issues
Rather than rigidly fixed views preventing differences
Diversities interacting highs/lows earthy/spiritual

Right/left polarities multiple ingredients stirring
The mixture of rigid recipes or remedies together
What it seems Thomas Aquinas did in his Summa
Offering diverse complexities as equally convincing
Conclusions around supposed church beliefs thus

Showing every angle related to the whole design
Distilling essences we sip see taste digest deliciously
Logical paragraphs questioning/responding about
Divinity's being beautifully expressed in succinct
Yet lengthy summaries making it impossible at

Least for me to figure which views Thomas held
As exclusively true since all his pros/cons make
Sense so I've no clue if he meant certain ones were
Dogmatic as each composed in lyrical seductively
Logical prose born by his loving heart mind soul

LAZARUS

Why was Jesus reluctant to raise Lazarus from
  the dead when his friends Mary and Martha came
crying for his help? Was it because he was not ready
  to reveal himself as possessing divine-like powers?
Some say he was so moved by the women's grief that
  he put aside personal plans and acted compassionately
so called Lazarus from the cave with warm welcoming
  words and wide-open arms along with his sisters . . .

MEMORY'S SHELTER

. . . sometimes it seems everything past and present
  feels interrelated with an earthy divine deliciousness
add what you wish to what you may at this moment
  most miss I toss in microscopic stuff pollen's honey
crystal particles melting sweetness in my tea rain drops
  sipped by sparrows on the maple leaves after winter
the garden glows with lavender & rosemary primroses
  by the front door memories serve as temporary shelters
so recover what we most miss toss in what you wish
  fun-filled times at home or vacations romantic moments
sprinkled as spice in our ordinary lives so welcomed
  showers after months of doubt during drought mini
miracles every day as rainbows over the horizon full
  moon crosses our bedspread your kind reach touches
me when in need may mine be felt by you especially if
  the going gets rough while we all look for reunions round
the table holding hands hugs galore singing Love songs

MINI RESURRECTIONS

. . . a field of waving wildflowers where a path parts in
  the distance as if answering our prayers a passageway
through loss as we come to a crossroad when it seems
  "an angel of mercy" appears out of the blue leading us

roundabout up down circling back to the beginning just
   going with the flow relearning love's around the corner
like finding lost letters of parents grandparents brothers
   sisters friends partners resaying their voices as we read
through winter's waning till suddenly it seems last year's
   lilies rise with forget-me-nots by the front door since earth's
thaw was happening little by little till time to hide Easter eggs
   for the grandkids who at last will be coming round again

EVE OF THE EPIPHANY

today's Eve of the Epiphany thanks to a friend's
   email saying the feast was changed a while ago
for convenience's sake regarding Christmas details

   I didn't know living on the fringes of the church's
liturgical life though I confess being forever grateful
   for deeply ingrained rituals of mystery setting

the scenes for belief in the magical wonder of God
   sending messengers including a child and angels
to earth making early awareness of sacred stories

   as normal even the story of Eden's couple falling
in love at first sight no parental approval needed
   no engagement announcements no debts incurred

except a soon-to-be major transgression called sinful
   by daring eat the doomed fruit so there they go
towards exile carrying a hubris sort of entitlement

   over all creation since placing blame for their fall
on a talking trickster who slipped into the scene
   as a friendly snake with sweet-sounding words

144

promising powers equal to or greater than their Creator
   so sugar-plum fantasies started dancing in their heads
raised to highest heavenly heights having dared taste

   the delicious apple who can say what harm can come
from such a simple deed unless the attitude of doing
   whatever you darn well wish no matter consequences

is partially the point i.e. wanting more than paradise
   rather the wish to possess total power the bottom line
dare I ask if anything has changed in human behavior

   over time yes no maybe a mixed bag promising
fantastic deliveries for a range of endless wishes cash
   credit fulfilling desires of possessing godlike powers

CHINESE ALCHEMY

During acupuncture daydreams fly from
   Streams within a cavern where Chi energy
Skips over obstacles washing away debris
   Rounding ridges reaching meridian islands
Relieving stagnation returning the Life force's
   Flow even if we first feared needles might
Hurt till the healer taught trust in the Tao's
   Wisdom discerning Nature's pulse places
Steadily strong gentle work underneath our
   Skin's covering so as to transform opposites
Into cooperative currents balancing reconciliation
   By discerning channels of communication
So surrendering "know it all" one-sided attitude
   Under ultraviolet light penetrating Nature's
Springs to action sending signals to toes up
   Again welcoming the East's ancient wisdom

CHAPEL BY THE SEASHORE

. . . may I recall long ago summers by the sea
watching a distant lighthouse blink on and off
    signaling a safe harbor for ships not far from
our convent's vacation home where I spent several
    summers singing with our sisters in a lovely chapel
by the seashore and a salty taste stayed on my tongue
    at communion what I felt was a tangible proof of
the Real Presence mixed in everything since ordinary
    things seemed charged with an earthy spirituality
even seaweed for cooking corn outside the kitchen door
    as belief in divinity mixed with a world filled with glory
while incense blew across the deck lingering later when
    we sipped wine at dinner and slept by open windows
as the surf rose and fell over and under dreams and desires

FAREWELL

A terra-cotta bowl overflows with geraniums
    by the garden gate. A fountain's humming.
Tomatoes, garlic, zucchini, chard and onions
    sizzle in olive oil. Red wine and fresh-baked
bread on the patio table. Awaiting your arrival.
    Joy I hardly hide. Breezes rustling linden leaves.
An Easter basket's multicolored pastel-coated eggs.
    Your footsteps echo along the stone path. Years
later a flood of memories. Remembering the stars
    set above the courtyard. Your incomparable smile,
brilliant intelligence and humility. Not one to seek
    attention, though brave in the face of controversy.
We enjoyed strawberries and cream for dessert with
    dark-roasted coffee. Church bells began ringing
round the corner. Time to say goodbye. Our paths
    diverged by the door. Never to meet again in such
a lovely setting. I prayed solo in chapel since sensing

your health was failing. Not devoted to discerning
destiny in the planets, yet suddenly a shooting star
through thick clouds at sunset the day you died.

URGING BALZAC ON A FRIEND

ages ago having fallen in love with Balzac in his books
I now recall the time I toured his garden by the Seine
then stood awestruck inside the small study where he
composed unforgettable characters writing at an intense
almost unbelievable pace thanks to drinking cup after
cup of black coffee throughout the night plus his self-
imposed deadline to complete the "Human Comedy"
before it was too late
                        so it was I tried convincing a friend T
to become a Balzac fan saying his portrayal of Eugénie
Grandet was a wonderful way of celebrating countless
"anonymous" women never known anywhere outside their
communities while he presented Eugénie as a magnificent
person who rather than become bitter by being betrayed by
the man she greatly loved she chose instead a life devoted
to caring for the poor and needy
                        thus I pleaded: "Why not try
Lost Illusions where Lucien's dreams, talents, loves, setbacks
stay memorably set in readers' hearts while astounded at
brave love for Lucien by a prostitute called Coralie
                        and even if
the first chapters about a printing press are boring the pace
will pick up making it impossible to put the book down."
                        did I
annoy by acting as if a press secretary for that author and
send my friend a Balzac book no memory of mailing such
and since that time we spoke of many things but I never again
mentioned that writer I adored though blest am I to live
not far from Rodin's bronzed Balzac at Stanford's museum

SALVADOR DALI'S CHRIST

Such a mysterious sign of the cross by Salvador
Dali portraying the beautiful Christ crucified on
   bare blond wood without a trace of blood face
unseen since turned sideways no nails visible
   not knowing how he is held suspended above
his beloved John who stands faithfully under
   a blue sky while voices whisper in the wings
wondering if art's a messenger at times making
   Transcendence tangible for us earthlings who
solo or together petition pray long for responses
   linking with loved ones across the great divide

FALLING IN LOVE WITHIN A FOREST
in memory of Joseph Grassi

. . . if death leaves us bereft can comfort come
   recalling scenes where our love first flourished
in New York's Seven Lakes region soon after we

left "religious life" returning to the world when
   love's dart at the start hit its mark as an angel
messenger named Eros happily happened to target

us no matter how or why delightful days in a tent
   by Lake Tiorati where we promised everlasting
love leaps years ahead as now I'm at a loss to shape

savor save our Saturday afternoons along glorious
   Palisades cliffs trails overlooking the Hudson River
as a photo shows me beaming in sunlight while sitting

on the hood of your car hands casually folded eyes
   expressing complete trust in whatever the future
has in store since a shared belief in sacramental signs

encouraging closeness within the forest of trees birds
    flowers fauna fountains streams fostering belief
that things will turn out well no matter our challenges

down the road even with leaps of faith across an abyss
    we will never give up hope in love lasting more than
a lifetime as is now my challenge recalling our first

leafy green wonders of a summer of our falling in love
    followed by transposing winter's inner sap into
magnificent colors of a new life with children playing

by the seashore so shall we stay forever lovers across
    the canopy of heaven earth's sweet-scented lavender
rising with bees spinning honeyed havens like stars

MINI MEDITATION, OUR FAMILY IN PARIS
thanks to Joseph, Eddie, Peter

A church door opened alongside a simple stall
    filled with flowers while across the square a mime
was performing by a café as a crowd was cheering
    and we joined in as bells chimed in the background
such a summer for our family seeing tasting smelling
    touching hearing magical things up close and lovely
so I've savored over years reviving that time and place
    of Paris one summer enjoying dinners outdoors along
a boulevard croissants and caffe latte for breakfast then
    for lunch cheese and baguette on a park bench plus
visiting the Mona Lisa together then riding bikes through
    the Versailles' forest attending Mass at Notre Dame
strolling along the Seine at night enjoying a mime's
    performance near our hotel as bells chimed beside
Saint-Germain-des-Prés where we lit candles . . .

DANTE IN EXILE, RAVENNA

". . . and when I was a stranger,
you took me in . . ." and so Dante exiled
from Florence took refuge here and there till
finally finding a home in Ravenna, where he
completed his "Paradiso"

                Was he alone there,
that is, without his wife, Emma? Were his sons
helpful, supportive? Was he recognized for
his gifts as a poet, or did he reside in Ravenna
incognito, pressing forward in his task to
complete his reunion with
Beatrice in paradise

                Was his long-ago memory
of her enough consolation to bring more than
hope, bring pleasure on lonely nights.

                Was he
refreshed by walks in the nearby pine forest?
Did he have loving friends nearby? What was
his relationship to the local parish?

                Did he dream
often of being welcomed back as poet laureate in
Florence, beloved city of birth, baptism, childhood,
marriage, where at age nine he fell in love on first
seeing Beatrice.

                We know from his translator,
Dorothy Sayers, he died from malaria contracted
when taking a short cut after a political mission in
Venice, that is cutting across infested swamps on his
Way back home to Ravenna.

                His concluding Paradiso
Cantos could not be found. Several years passed till
one day his son searching his father's rooms he happened
upon the final verses hidden within a wall alcove.

                Perhaps

Dante felt a premonition before that trip to Venice since he
hid his concluding lines without telling anyone.

Blessed
are we his readers over centuries with such magnificent
concluding verses revealing the heavenly Rose vision
where Beatrice resides . . .

VAYA CON DIOS
in memory of my brother Richie Cook

Moon rising. Owls calling over the ridge.
    Foxes trotting in brambles. Sweet scented
pine resin sticks to my fingers. I remove
    twigs from my hair. Stars act as guides
revealing the road through darkness. We
    hugged "goodbye" as if saying "till we
meet again," though I felt it was a final
    farewell. Your wife Loretta and I held
your hands. We three praying the familiar
    Our Father. Next morning I walked
once more up the road round the edge '
    of the lake. Fresh buds on every bush.
My nephew Terence ready to drive me to
    the airport. Niece Tara standing beside
the open door, eyes full of tears, knowing
    her great-souled father would be passing
over as the forest he loved was beginning to
    bloom. We shared belief without saying
so in a Divine plan working in wings behind
    the scene transforming loss into eternal Life . . .

WE ARE NOT ALONE

at first I failed to notice the beauty surrounding me
    instead gazed at the ground wishing someone would
tap me on the shoulder and say: "Keep believing that in

151

time all will be well again" but no voices heard, till I
entered memory's sanctuary so saw light swimming in
an open ceiling as doves circled and hosts of honeybees

left trails of black and golden pollen dust as they hummed
round the shepherd's forehead while lifting a lamb to
his heart saying: "You are not alone" as I heard the soft

"Baa, baa, baa" rise to the rafters as I asked for our wounded
earth's healing and he smiled offering bread and wine we
tasted together as others joined round the table while a dove

flew down swift as a shooting star from the sky settling close
enough to hear cooing and see fiery eyes blinking kindly
though a thunderstorm roared nearby with bolts of lightning

rain gave a benediction of abundance to our drought-plagued
land then night's protective blanket of sleep settled over
everything till we heard voices of children laughing at dawn

HOLY WEEK

Oh help me learn humility
not be ashamed to be like lilies
of the valley bent over in storms
longing for family and friends
trying to trust comfort comes in
unexpected "angels of mercy"
appearing out of the blue sent by
You through thick and thin times
of need although lackadaisical in
my deeds and omissions I trust
good intentions count in sprinkling
forgiveness generously again so
place petitions for all in need before
Your loving gaze trusting care exists

for each none excluded today tomorrow
linking our lives again brought together
   to beginnings wherever they may be
mine being a Brooklyn parish's radiantly
   dark interior where I tasted Your manna
for Life's journey sailing rough seas seeking
   safe harbor You steer at the helm as I hum
the hymn learned long ago singing solo
   sheltering in place I raise my rusty voice
with a choir of resurrected loved ones:
         Alleluia! Alleluia! Alleluia!

ROME WITH JOE
in memory of Joseph Grassi

Remembering our taxi ride from the airport that
hot August afternoon, windows wide open, wind
blowing my hair as the driver whizzed round ancient
Roman gates, leaving us off at Via Marguta, after
a nap we climbed the Spanish Steps, ah dinner at

"The Ramp," wine, pungent tomato basil pasta,
salad and vanilla torte sprinkled with chocolate,
then we strolled the Borghese garden ramparts
overseeing the brooding dome of Saint Peter's
in the distance, this your first time back in Rome

after decades, we visited sites of your studies
at the Gregorian and Pontifical Biblical Institute,
the latter refusing entrance to the garden as
the receptionist said: "only priests allowed"
though in fluid Italian you explained being

an alumnus, no difference, she likely guessed
I was your wife meaning you're no longer
a priest, while the Maryknoll House, where

you lived for 3 years, and they warmly welcomed
us! while later I wondered whether you felt

"the loss" of being a priest as painful, never
expressing regrets, since you taught Scripture,
after the major seminary, at the Jesuits' Santa
Clara University thanks to Fr. Ted Mackin,
who wished a married clergy was welcomed

by the church, so he happily hired you, though
two prominent Catholic universities at that time
actually sent letters responding to your application:
"We do not hire laicized priests to teach in our
Religious Studies Department." I wanted to send

these letters to the National Catholic Reporter,
but you said "Better not, since other universities
may put obstacles to my being hired even at SCU."
We prayed at Saint John Lateran where you recalled
when you climbed the pilgrims' stairs on your knees,

this said while we strolled under plane trees on our
way to Santa Maria Maggiore, stopping for a gelato
at a sidewalk café, where you described a miraculous
snowfall ages ago on August 15 at this site, same day
as your mother's birthday . . . her dying young made

it possible for you to follow your dream of being
a priest, since at her funeral your father finally gave
his permission for you to enter the seminary, saying:
"This was her wish for you" so intertwined lives
within this city's history, yours, ours and the church

we've loved, as with Ted Mackin studying here as
a priest then decades later a postcard from Rome
celebrating his honeymoon. (Sadly dying three years

later.) Thankfully you lived longer, now I'm a widow
recalling that long ago blessedly beautiful summer.

ROCKAWAY TO LINDA MAR BEACH PACIFICA
in memory of Joseph Grassi

Was that your spirit appearing along the crest
   of this wintry green hill overlooking the ocean
rising gentle up-sweeps wings widespread so
   close I could hear the feathers beating as my heart
beat faster too recalling our first sighting of a heron
   when we hiked this zigzag path from Rockaway
Beach to the crest alongside Rt 1 before descending
   to Linda Mar State Beach where the great bird landed
by willows then stepping slowly bending each leg back
   soon a springing flight slow-motion flapping over
the hill turning towards those ocean caves you so loved . . .

AVEBURY REFRAIN AGAIN

We came in late morning near the end
of October, when the light was faint as
clouds floated overhead and fog filled

the moors, while we were walking down
a slippery slope from the car park. A small
village close by and to right rising below

in soft green glory, a burial mound barrow.
Traffic humming, birds calling in chestnut
trees and the swishing sound of wild grasses

in the wind beside the smiling sarsen stones
as if saying: "Come close, confide your secrets,
share dreams." No gate or fence keeping us

apart, no sign saying: "Keep your distance."
Only access, acceptance, affection each to
each, one for all and all for one without

discrimination, a deeply grounded "being"
as silvery gentle flecks in large gray stones
released flashes of blue ribbons across tiny

pools of watery crevices leaning on ledges
that caught momentary shadows of clouds
heading west. No one else sighted. Just us

among these creatures together under sun, moon,
stars, rain, drought, heat, cold, temperate times
as though traveling beyond this border without

leaving, close to high heaven, deeply set side by
side in earth, spanning centuries without preaching,
simply practicing a genuine habitual welcome

while their souls whirl with mysteries and prayers
that emit sparkling energies, rejoicing as children
climb on their shoulders, laughing and singing . . .

MINIATURE ALLELUIAS

Let me learn trust like lilies of the valley
    that Spring's resurrection time shall dawn

so I will stand strong again with willows
    waving in warmer weather beside

loved ones I miss since sheltering solo
    in place for months though blest with

a home plus angels of mercy for help
   with grocery deliveries and best of all

when weather allows social-distancing
   visits in the backyard with family so it

is a perennial rediscovery of the wonderful
   Being birthing this world hiding in flowers

trees sky sea friends families communities
   of every kind no ledger of deeds no marks

for falling short no preaching perfection since
   unconditional Love means what the words

say though many may including me falter by
   daring to impute dark motives to those whom

we disagree with on issues dear to our hearts
   sadly forgetting mercy's roots in reconciliation

seeds planted as showers bring back flowers lilies
   reappear by the path beside my door as a chorus

singing miniature alchemical *alleluias* as "I bend
   down in humble adoration How great Thou art"*
   (* sung by Elvis Presley at his final concert)

THE KISS OF PEACE

   Let's consider Catholic belief in forgiveness prevailing
at the end of life if a person confesses regret with or
   without a priest present not fearing "fire & brimstone"
feelings of hell since mercy's magnified don't get me
   wrong I'm not apologizing for leading a life without
caring about others but who knows another soul's

struggles isn't it comforting to recall the sympathetic
One who sees knows understands each and all offering
  "unconditional love" as a birthright so may we try
follow forgiveness as a practice with mercy by our side
  rejoicing as rainbows rise after storms helping peace
and reconciliation prevail while we bow across the aisle
  to friends and strangers in a ritual Kiss of Peace . . .

MEDITATION ON TURNER'S TABERNACLE
in memory of Joseph Grassi

1.

He brushed away tiredness and held his hand high
  in hope of gently applying a sheen of gold leaf
to the canvass as if a transcendent moment adding
  rusty edges to quiet places marked by grief as
the green hills rose almost to the sky and below
  a long curving cliff to set caves and beaches for
hiding dreams and secrets while to the side he
  placed an ancient oak breathing veils of steam
in an early Spring morning after a long cold winter
  seeing the sun rise through clouds in the east
where flocks of beautiful birds came so close to
  rubbing each other's feathers as they migrated
over towns fields mountains cities villages mirrored
  in windows of intimacy since guided by a shared
singular inner compass calling them back home . . .

2.

so it seemed seeing your courageous calm in those
  last years months weeks days hours facing the final
journey serenely at peace the way seemingly Turner's
  final paintings held sacred human earthly spiritual
desires dreams dawns strongly faintly flickering
  flames of sunlight with gorgeous dark clouds over
landscapes cities and seas the way we witnessed

158

together his final paintings exhibited at the Tate
. . . awestruck we stood before such astounding beauty
of what seemed a tabernacle's sacred space housing
his soul's glorious culminating works in a symphony
beyond belief but felt alongside all as if in paradise . . .

PARADISE RE-FOUND

. . . a universal, yet particular experience,
seeking for signs that we are not alone, even
as I am now composing this poem in a café

after reading Milton's brilliant "Paradise Lost,"
composed when blind, perhaps prompting his
empathy for Lucifer and the fallen followers

by identifying with their loss of heavenly light,
wondering if he questioned God's eternal
punishment as appropriate, since an undertone

of "way too harsh" permeates his writings,
thus a questioning of Hell's unchangeable
dreadful consequences for a single act of

rebellion, yet 1600's British belief in Hell's
existence existed, except as a loophole in
Catholicism's view that any act of regret even

at death's doorway was granted forgiveness
including so-called "mortal sins," thus erasing
crimes or misdemeanors committed by anyone

seems an empathetic imprint on Catholic souls,
though difficult finding such beliefs expressed
among moderns, yet some of us persist believing

in blessings bestowed lavishly by Divine mercy for
one and all, no matter past or present offenses if
a person expresses regret and calls for forgiveness

WALKING THIS BEAUTIFUL EARTH

redwoods amazing survival from firestorms
mentoring humans how to go let go go with
the flow reviving life after loss lichen shields
waving wands of survival salamanders sun-
bathing again on logs seeds sprouting in rocks
streams spawning salmon as we dare reimagine
taking trails uphill over mountain crests close
to clouds down around the lake find a field
to roll in high hay sniff buttercups watch a fox's
rippling burnt-sienna fur fern fans proliferating
on the forest's floor woodpeckers busy back at
work oak grove awakening legends of Arthur
Galahad Guinevere Merlin's magical kingdom
encouraging daydreams over a ridge or take
a new bend in the road sap pulse beneath palms
when we touch a mother madrone where we
confide our struggles with weeping willows hug
each other round oaks savor wild strawberries
surprised by poppies pushing through stones
eastern woods where we first met thrive in our
memory out west till death do us part and beyond
as we've rejoiced walking this beautiful earth . . .

BRING ME STRINGS TO SING

oh, bring me strings to sing Your praises,

settle down close to the ground, listen to plants

purring, see separate paths converging, broken

bridges rebuilt, scattered nests restored, uprooted

plants find refuge in softened soil while I lie down

with you in a field under a night filled with moon

and stars, welcoming dawn in each other's arms

SURPRISES WHEN LEAST EXPECTED

. . . surprises when least expected, as I find a note
    from a long ago friend in the mailbox, a neighbor
waves Hello, familiar voices of family coming into
    the garden, such joy it seems even the lavender
and rosemary sing "so great to see you," high as a kite
    the joy felt in their presence, then two small books
seem to fall into my hands when most needed, one
    by Freud the other by Jung, composed near the end
of their long lives, different as they were, yet convergent
    in heartfelt calls for tolerance, humility, compassion,
appeals to go easy on oneself and every one else . . .

LAMB OF GOD

Lamb of God teach us to turn towards earth's
    plentiful plants seeds nuts so set free all
creatures as yourself plus cows pigs chickens

    turkeys rabbits kept in suffering bondage for
slaughter just to feed us humans as we preach
    for the climate change cause yet continuing

to consume animals who were kept in cages for
    our appetites worse by far if creatures spend
their lives in factory farms overproducing as

many as possible for profits thus increasing
methane gases highest polluters of earth's
atmosphere while mother earth watches her

beloved creatures killed for humans such as this
profoundly beautiful being whose kin deserve
saving to lead long lives not so surprising that
Christ   Lamb of God   Good Shepherd

REFRAIN

Lamb of God who takes away
our fears, who absolves doubts
binding wounds and teaching
compassion, hear our prayer

Lamb of God, Son of Sophia, who
walks beside the trails we take,
crossing fields, finding us lost on
night journeys, hear our prayer

ADORABLE NAMES

Has your name changed over years?
Were you once called Apollo?
Guardian spirit touching down
feathered feet on earth the way
Mercury might? Or simply a special
guardian angel assigned at birth?
Who will dare say today they've
seen you once more running to
the crossroads with a compass and
wise directions for the journey.
Oh be again present in our hours
of loss doubt and confusion. Be
assured we'll welcome you in any

disguise you desire recognized by
kind ways with or without wings. . .

GOOD SHEPHERD FLOCKS

Lambs are licking his hands and drinking
water from his palms as a stream pours
down the cliff over his head and shoulders
while he laughs looking far across the field
searching and calling for any lost sheep and
when found letting each one know He cares
by lifting and holding them close to His heart
through howling storms or sweltering summers
He offers food and shelter to sleep with warm
wooly bodies close by since none are slaughtered

MERCURY

Mercury's splendid sight beneath the moon these
    Autumn nights gloriously steady and seemingly
still as if stopped in meditation not yet running back
    east confining this glow to our western sky where
we still hold sparks of summer's green good warmth
    filling fields of wildflowers so we may feel kinship
to the heavens as our hearts form constellations of
    attachments along the highways and byways since
Love like Eros aims an arrow at us pulling diversity
    together in a promised affinity even as we face
mortality daring to seal our Life's path with others
    traveling like Mercury's dear destiny into night
over the Pacific yet rising again at dawn in the east
    sometimes streaking fast or seemingly slowed
down through Autumn and Winter into Spring's
    reassuring sprouts by our earthy feet as above . . .

DARKNESS GOES INTO DAWN'S WARM ARMS

A faint light spreads as darkness goes into dawn's
    warm arms and off to the side auburn branches

of manzanitas melt lingering frost as March tosses
    off winter's sheltering blankets after months of

hibernation soothed by a hawk's wings flying low
    so see up close a brilliant red ring woven within

a fan of lustrous black tail feathers as if brushed
    by visibly sacred chorus of countless blessings

swaying inside orange poppies that bloom in
    a burnt-sienna boulder as if earth's deep down

desires rose after months in hibernation at last let
    loose in a fresh-found grandeur we too rejoice

together bend down to touch tender pussy willow
    wands over milkweed and yarrow alongside

the ocean trail above where people play on the beach
    surfers glide over breakers while beyond the crests

whales spout their perpetual springs of joy on their
    journey from Alaska back to birthing waters in Baja

STONEHENGE, SARSEN STONES SMILE

. . . while the sun goes down in western waters
    the stones settle into a blanket of darkness time

to rest till dawn slips through crevices warming
    under around above as we too far from loved

ones sheltering in place during a pandemic as
  an adage ages ago "whatever gets you through

the night" we can imagine a calm garden circle
  with birds zooming so close we hear their wings

flapping on a warm afternoon while we relax in
  a haven of gentle giants redwoods pines stones

whatever you prefer bees humming in heather see
  a golden path of daffodils in the middle so we stroll

round ancient ancestors our once original together
  seeds to earth's eggs beginnings literal legendary

no matter we go with the flow of Life's amazing
  companions Autumn apples summer corn winter

acorns such bewitching beauty in human faces to
  behold wild irises almond trees in flower babies

arriving kittens puppies fauns fledglings a lively
  cha-cha or calm chorus *when you walk through a storm*

kneeling down beside troubled waters a rainbow bridge
  below rain clouds showering our parched landscapes

who knows completely the history who carried such
  stones how hard the labor   what long distances

difficult circumstances yet we humans join butterflies
  birds migrations *hope springs eternal* as we set welcome

signs in our hearts for Love's reunion wherever possible
  gardens apartments parks homes again together at last

A VIRTUAL BOW OF THANKS
for friends and family past, present, future

Hibernating indoors candles burn bright
   out of storms the way my poetry stays
in files few see though dear ones support
   perhaps not realizing how crucial they
are sustaining my work from beginning
   to end I try recalling the gospel message
how various gifts are equally worthwhile
   since all labor contributes to the whole
as the cook during a retreat pleased when
   monks and guests enjoy the vegetable
soup salad and blueberries harvested from
   bushes warmed under the sun so may each
person's work be valued as I bow my thanks
   to the kindness you've granted me over years

About the Author:

Carolyn Grassi, born and raised in Brooklyn, New York, lives in the San Francisco Bay Area. She was a member of the Maryknoll Sisters and graduated from Brooklyn College CUNY with a B.A. in Political Science and Education, an M.A. and M.P.A. from San Jose State University in Political Science (thesis: *Individual Freedom in Hegel's Philosophy of the State*). She has taught Philosophy and Political Science at California community colleges, led workshops in Creative Writing and given readings at the San Jose Poetry Center, Books Inc. NYC, Black Oak Books, Smith College and Yale. She has published several books of poetry and her poems have appeared in various journals. Carolyn and her late husband, Joseph Grassi, co-led workshops in Scripture and the Arts for the Osher Institute at Santa Clara University.

Carolyn Grassi is a recipient of an Ingram Merrill Foundation Grant Award and was nominated for a Pushcart Prize in Poetry by the late Harry Ford of Knopf. She gave a weekend workshop on Wagner's The Ring Cycle for the C.G. Jung Institute of San Francisco and a presentation on Creative Imagination for the Analytical Psychology Club of San Francisco. She is a long-time member of the San Jose Poetry Center, Amnesty International, the ACLU, and the Sierra Club.

"Some random reflections called up by Carolyn Grassi's poetry reading last evening (1984). It revealed a very rich, very intense inner life; also, that she has been undergoing a process of profound self-discovery as a woman and as a human being. I think that must be what she means when speaking of "meditation through writing." Although imagined through female experience, for me the poems point to a depth beyond masculinity and femininity to universal human experience. Openness begets openness, depth resonates with depth beyond gender. That made it particularly meaningful. It

167

revealed a great awe and reverence for some of the deepest of human experiences—beautifully captured in tender and delicate wording. I saw her shedding light and love for us on our human experience."

Peter Michelozzi, career counselor, board member Habitat
  for Humanity, Santa Cruz County and IF Community

> "Ole Shakespeare can our teacher be
> In politics and poetry.
> Those who, in these darker times,
> Doubt this can be,
> Need only listen
> To Grassi."

by the late Dr. John Wettergreen, Political Science,
San Jose State University

Postscript

HOMAGE TO THE LITTLE ONES
in thanks to the Sisters of Charity,
and in memory of all the girls who lived at
Saint Joseph's Home, Brooklyn, New York

As a teenager, I used to volunteer at a home for girls. I'd
ride the Myrtle Avenue El from my high school, which was
near the Brooklyn Bridge. One day a girl was riding the train
too. She was wearing a school uniform same as mine. As we
got off at the same stop, I asked: "Are you going to volunteer
at Saint Joseph's Home too?" She replied: "No, I live there."

I was assigned to help with the little ones, ages three to five.
Ms. X, the woman in charge, was strict and rarely smiled. She
would shout: "Time for showers!" I'd bring five girls at
a time into the large bathroom, then help each one undress,
and lift them on to a high shower platform. They shivered,
either from cold, fear or both. Ms. X used a powerful hose to
clean them off, while shouting: "Turn around. Bend over."

Only when I came on a Sunday afternoon, did I realize this
home was not exactly an orphanage. Ms. X told me to get
the girls ready for Visiting Hour. I helped them put on
a favorite dress and brushed their hair. Excited little voices
filled the locker room. "Today my Mommy is coming!"
"My Daddy is coming too!" Then they waited on their cots.
A few names were called to the guest room: "Margaret"
"Catherine" "Grace." Three or four had a visitor among
twenty girls.

Next all changed into everyday clothes to go outside on
the cement playground, where they'd play tag, take turns
on swings, jump rope, or throw a rubber ball. I overheard
some girls telling each other that I was "their sister."

Whenever the young Sister of Charity entered The Nursery, the girls ran to hug her. She spoke gently, calling each by their name. bending down and kissing every child. As the dinner bell rang, Sister said: "I will come later, tuck you in bed, and say goodnight."

Sometimes I stayed to serve dinner in a small nearby room. Ms. X insisted: "Be quiet or this nice girl, who comes to help, will not come back if you misbehave!" My heart ached seeing four girls at each table eating dinner in total silence. I'd wave goodbye as the nearby girls reached out to touch me.

Heading home, I walked down deserted streets to the bus. Eventually my Dad said: "I know you love to visit that home, but unless you get a friend to come along, you can't continue. It's too risky coming home alone, taking two buses, especially when it's dark in the winter." None of my friends' parents allowed them to come with me in what they called "an unsafe neighborhood."

A final goodbye visit, though to this day I carry guilt about not returning and still remember several names and faces of those precious little ones. I've prayed that Ms. X became kindlier, but who can know what another person's private life is like. Who am I to judge, since I had a loving family waiting for me at home each day.

Thankfully, the Sisters of Charity acted as mothers for all these girls from birth through high school, and perhaps even longer, while welcoming their parents, who probably were teenagers. (Thanks to the Sisters of Saint Joseph (Brentwood, Long Island, New York) my teachers at Saint Joseph's High School, Brooklyn, who encouraged their students to volunteer in underserved communities.)

Made in the USA
Las Vegas, NV
14 October 2021